LANDSCAPES AND DESIRE

LANDSCAPES AND DESIRE

Revealing Britain's Sexually Inspired Sites

CATHERINE TUCK
PHOTOGRAPHS BY ALUN BULL

SUTTON PUBLISHING

First published in the United Kingdom in 2003 by
Sutton Publishing Limited · Phoenix Mill
Thrupp · Stroud · Gloucestershire · GL5 2BU

Text copyright © Catherine Tuck, 2003

Photographs copyright © Alun Bull, 2003

British Library Cataloguing in Publication Data
A catalogue record for this book is available from the British Library.

ISBN 0-7509-2939-1

Title page photograph: the Mudmaid, Lost Gardens of Heligan, Cornwall.

Typeset in 12/16 pt Perpetua.
Typesetting and origination by
Sutton Publishing Limited.
Printed and bound in England by
J.H. Haynes & Co. Ltd, Sparkford.

Contents

CONTENTS

Acknowledgements

Numerous individuals gave generously of their time, ideas and support during the creation of *Landscapes and Desire* and we would like to take this opportunity to offer our sincerest thanks to all of you.

The first thank you must go to the author's parents, Gwen and David Tuck, who entered into the spirit of our work with great enthusiasm and made countless emergency dashes around the countryside to check references or the lengths of phalluses. A huge thank you is due to Ann Gadsby for patience over Alun's many prolonged absences and for help in organising the photographic archive. To Peter Stanier, also, for sharing a house with the moods and mess of a writer and for early morning lifts to the airport. We are deeply grateful to professional colleagues for their ideas and contributions: especially David McOmish, Steve Cole, Wayne Cocroft, Peter Topping, Dave Went, Chris Dunn, Keith Blood, Adam Menuge, Dave Field, John and Liz Whitbourn, Danielle Devlin, Stratford Halliday and Tom Clare. We are indebted, also, to those specialists who have added their academic experience in commenting upon the text: Peter Topping (again), Tony Wilmot, Noël James and Moraig Brown.

For providing access to information we would like to thank Angela Gannon of the Royal Commission on the Ancient and Historical Monuments of Scotland, Georgina Plowright of the Corstopitum Roman Museum and Alison Brisby at Castle Howard. For allowing access to sites we are grateful to the Lost Gardens of Heligan and Sue and Peter Hill, the creators of the Mudmaid, to Douglas Paterson at Mine Howe, John Comino-James, Tim Shaw and Peter Hempel at the Eden Project, Sir Edward Dashwood, Louise Hudson at Alton Towers, the wonderful lady in whose grounds the Newton Stones stand, staff at Maes Howe, the Vindolanda Trust, and the staff at Turoe Farm. We would like to say a big thank you to Dúchas Heritage Service, the National Trust, English Heritage, and all site custodians who have helped us with access or tracing obscure features, especially Paul Bentley at Cheters, John Heslop at Housesteads, John Farquharson at Lansdown Tower, the staff at the Senhouse Museum in Maryport, the Bath Roman baths, Fishbourne Roman palace and the Sussex Archaeological Society, and to the Barbara Hepworth Museum and Sculpture Garden in St Ives.

Thanks, too, to Steven Tuck for master-minding the book website, to Lori Ballard for help taking pictures (and for sleeping in a field) on a weekend of extreme weather, and to Phillip for trying to fix us up with a boat on the Thames. We would also like to thank our pilots Justin Cox, Elizabeth Barton and Andy Southorn for getting us off the ground for the aerial photography.

The Tourist Information Board get our rapturous applause for their army of wonderfully helpful staff as does Bill Giles for his excellent web-based weather forecasts. We are grateful to Cambridge City Library for the loan of a huge box of Ordnance Survey Landranger maps.

Our grateful thanks to Rab Carrington Ltd, Sheffield, for their help with expedition equipment, to Ray Clarke and staff at Streamline Colour Labs, Cambridge, for their support and careful film-handling throughout the project and to the Association of Historical and Fine Art Photography.

We would like to say a big thank you to the team at Sutton Publishing who have worked on *Landscapes and Desire*, especially our editors Christopher Feeney and Matthew Brown.

Lastly we would like to express our appreciation to our friends and families for their magnificent support, including anyone not named here in person but who has contributed to the creation of *Landscapes and Desire*.

TECHNICAL NOTES

The sites contained within *Landscapes and Desire* were visited on a series of expeditions around the British Isles during which we travelled close to 30,000 miles by foot, sea, air and car. These trips – for the purposes of researching and photographing each place – were undertaken between autumn 2001 and summer 2003, a period which encompassed one of the wettest years on record.

Careful planning ensured that we avoided the worst of the weather and a large dose of good fortune provided us with some of the most stunning light, clouds and skies that this part of the world has to offer. Catching the best quality light on film sometimes took moments – but more often days – of patient waiting. We spent many hours in the company of sunrise and sunset living by the same light that would have been so important to our ancestors. Waking at 3.00 a.m. at mid summer in the Northern Isles in order to be ready to photograph before sunrise made for spectacular but very long working days.

We lived in the most sumptuous outdoor clothing made and supplied by Rab Carrington Ltd, of Sheffield, and caught up on sleep in their beautifully warm sleeping bags. So that we could be in position and ready to photograph at dawn, accommodation was, by necessity, under canvas. For nearly two years, home was one of a range of superb Terra Nova tents. These were pitched wherever the photography dictated – from extreme mountainsides in winter to a not-so-extreme adventure playground in Ireland. Cooking in remote spots was the only option and for this we used various Mountain Safety Research stoves – all of which worked faultlessly.

The images in this book were shot using only natural available light (with the exception of some interiors) on Fuji Velvia ISO 50 and Provia 100F (36×24 small format and 6×7 medium format) film. The main camera used was a Contax with Carl Zeiss lenses but some work was shot on a Canon EOS. A Voightländer range finder was used for extreme wide angle photography and the medium format work was done on a Mamiya RZ 67. All of the photographs were taken with the aid of a tripod (with the exception of the aerial work and a couple where the viewpoint was too precipitous). No coloured filters were used but Lee graduated neutral density filters were employed when the difference in exposure between the foreground and sky was beyond the range of the film.

For further information about the making of *Landscapes and Desire*, forthcoming exhibitions and related projects you are invited to visit www.landscapes-and-desire.co.uk.

The Mound of Venus lies at the centre of West Wycombe's landscaped female form: 'For the entrance to it is the same entrance by which we all come into the world, and the door is what some wits have called the "Door of Life"' – John Wilkes.

CHAPTER ONE

From Eden to Eternity

SEX IS NOT A MERE PHYSIOLOGICAL TRANSACTION . . . IT PERVADES ART
AND IT PRODUCES ITS SPELLS AND MAGIC . . . IT DOMINATES IN FACT
ALMOST EVERY ASPECT OF CULTURE.

BRONISLAW MALINOWSKI

West Wycombe Park in Buckinghamshire is a quintessentially English stately home set in four hundred luxurious acres of country estate. For centuries the seat of the Dashwood family, it was the residence, nearly three hundred years ago, of the notorious hedonist and founder of the infamous Hell-Fire Club, Sir Francis Dashwood. Although these grounds are now open to the public, the guidebook does not quite tell the whole story. Thousands of visitors come each year to experience this elegant and historic place and most will leave without realising the covertly erotic nature of what they have seen. For West Wycombe Park is the scene of one of the eighteenth century's most salacious legacies.

Within a woodland clearing, a rounded grassy knoll, sun-dappled and veiled in a gossamer covering of white cow parsley, rises from the green carpet of early summer. A stone façade at the base of the mound spreads to either side revealing a narrow oval slit just large enough to slip through. This is the entrance to a subterranean grotto – a small, damp cavern beneath the mound. Surmounting the temple is a statue of Venus, the Roman goddess of love. The symbolism in this secluded folly is unmistakably erotic but any doubt as to the carnal nature of its design is dispelled by the temple's location at West Wycombe. Dashwood is reputed to have erected the Mound of Venus at the centre of a private landscape of sculpted mounds and hollows, curving pathways and parterres that was laid out to be daringly evocative of the naked female form.

These gardens were created at the height of a Georgian fashion for suggestive landscapes. Such risqué endeavours were not only tolerated, but also highly desired by a genteel society eager for titillation, and their symbolism would not have been lost amidst the blushings of a classically educated audience. But this libidinous aristocrat was by no means the first to express a passion for the female form outdoors. Although the eighteenth century would go down in history as an unparalleled time of sexual freedom, others before Dashwood had felt moved to celebrate nature's eternal forces on an open-air stage. Dashwood was, in fact, following a tradition that can be traced back over five thousand years to the builders of Britain's Stone Age monuments and temples.

As an enduring element of human life, sex has been acknowledged by world religions variously as a path to spiritual wisdom or the road to eternal damnation. It has occupied anthropologists and psychologists for decades and as a source of pleasure or power its variations are, perhaps, unlimited. A word has even been derived from the Latin *caelebs* to describe a state of existence devoid of it. When it comes to sex, Malinowski, it seems, was not exaggerating. For as long as there has been 'society', people have explored and expressed their sexuality through the various media available to them. The passing millennia may have seen carved stones and painted murals superseded by digital and celluloid recording, but there has always been the workable canvas of the landscape. So we should not be surprised to discover that the countryside of Britain and Ireland is bursting with an incredibly diverse array of sites created in recognition or celebration of human sexuality. We simply need to know what to look for. In order to understand some of the background to these places, it may be helpful to examine what must be Britain's most blatant sexual landscape feature.

Approaching the small Dorset town of Cerne Abbas from the north, attention is invariably distracted by a spur of high ground rising to the north-east where, carved into the gleaming chalk, is the unmistakable outline of an enormous white phallus. It is attached to the sixty-metre tall outline of a naked man whose immodest depiction not only dominates the entire hillside but has also been the centre of explicit fertility rites for longer than anyone can recall.

The Cerne Abbas Giant is a familiar image in the British landscape. His massive, gnarled club and priapic manhood have ensured him plenty of interest from inquisitive tourists, modern pagans and from copulating couples hoping to invoke some latent power of conception. At seven metres in length, his gargantuan erect member has gained the Cerne Abbas Giant a certain prominence. Numerous publicity stunts have focused on the outsized genitalia including the overnight addition, in August 2002, of a colossal condom by groups promoting family planning awareness. But not everyone is keen to appreciate the figure in all his naked glory. As recently as 1994, objections to his nudity were voiced through letters to a national newspaper campaigning to have the giant decently covered. Concerns over the indecency of the figure were evidently an issue, though, long before these moral machinations.

In 1888 and again in 1902, the Ordnance Survey updated maps of the area surrounding Cerne Abbas. The giant, on both editions, had been completely emasculated leaving the simple dotted outline of a person. We have to suspect that this was censorship as the result of cultural sensitivity since, in the nineteenth century, the figure clearly had strong sexual associations. On the first day of May, in continuation of an ancient springtime celebration, a maypole was still being erected in an adjacent prehistoric enclosure known as the Trendle. Women who were experiencing difficulty conceiving would sometimes sit or make love on the giant's phallus in the belief that, through the process of sympathetic magic, his evident virility would affect their own reluctant bodies.

Society often holds conflicting views on such activities, and references to these patently pagan superstitions were greatly discouraged by the

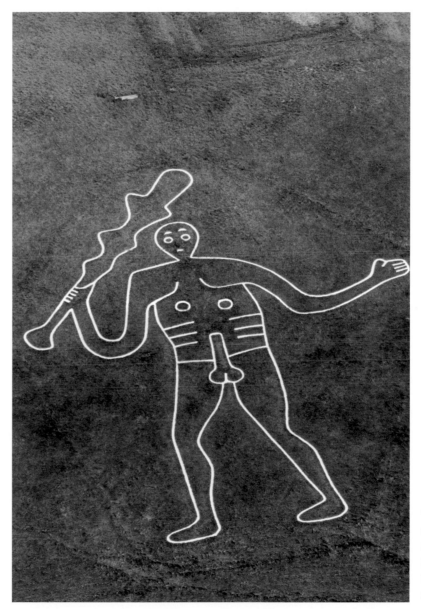

The origins of the rampant Cerne Abbas Giant remain a mystery but for centuries he has been the focus for fertility rites.

Christian church. Without being constantly renewed by freshly cutting and impacting the chalk, the giant would soon become overgrown with grass and disappear. 'Scourings' were traditionally carried out every seven years to preserve the pristine appearance of the figure, but a local vicar once temporarily vetoed their continuation because, he said, they represented an adherence to pagan superstition. Perhaps he had good reason to be concerned, because it seems to have been as the result of a scouring early in the twentieth century that the giant's navel was subsumed into a two metre augmentation of his penis.

Today the green headland is known as Giant's Hill but this term was only recently bestowed upon the site. The origins of the figure are, in fact, a complete mystery. Archaeologists and historians are still debating whether he is the work of a seventeenth-century politician or prehistoric farmers. The first written record of the Cerne Abbas Giant appears in a letter written in 1751 by the Dorset historian John Hutchins. In this he states a belief that the figure is a relatively recent addition to the hillside although it seems he may have been referring to one of the scourings that so offended the local vicar. But villagers at this time had their own explanation for the figure who stared down at them from his rounded flank of chalk downland. Eighteenth-century folklore tells of a Danish giant who ravaged the countryside around

Cerne Abbas but who made a mistake that would prove to be fatal. After eating his fill of villagers' sheep, he lay down on the hillside to sleep off his meal. According to the story, enraged villagers cut off his head, drawing round his body as a warning to any other outsized marauders.

William Stukeley, one of Britain's most prominent antiquarians, was not convinced by this rural yarn. Writing in 1764, he maintained that the figure was an ancient depiction – a classical god such as Hercules – and this explanation endures as one of the plausible theories surrounding the origins of the giant. Interestingly, a finely crafted estate map drawn four years later suffers from none of the modesty of the Victorian cartography. The gigantic genitals are shown in full frontal detail, though the penis is depicted in a less rampant state than it appears today. Whether this was to conform to some sexual etiquette at the time is debatable, but it is clear that the outline of the figure has been altered over time.

The seventeenth and eighteenth centuries were a period of unprecedented sexual frankness. A tradition of celebrating human sexuality in the great outdoors was pursued with enthusiasm by numerous wealthy and eccentric landowners. Classical culture was enjoying a renaissance in Britain and the contributions of individuals such as Sir Francis Dashwood set the tone for what was deemed acceptable. In the

The chalk outline of the figure has been altered over time: in the early 1900s the giant's navel was subsumed into a two-metre augmentation of his penis.

seventeenth century the estates around the foot of Giant's Hill were home to the Member of Parliament for Dorchester, Lord Denzil Holles. Some accounts attribute the creation of the giant to this fervent royalist, either as a satirical or even personal comment – or as a daring practical joke. Apparently Holles may have visited the Roman remains at Corstopitum in Northumberland, where a stone effigy of the club-wielding Hercules is strikingly similar to the giant at Cerne Abbas.

The contemporary landscaped gardens of Holles's estate, containing fine parterres and elaborate water features, may also be significant. Surviving now only as grassy lumps and hollows in a field full of docile cows, it is possible to discern two circular mounds between which a section of straight canal extends. This arrangement, viewed from a prospect mound in the corner of the garden, echoes perfectly the genitals of the giant on the hillside above and may have been created by Holles in replication of the chalk figure.

For several hundred years prior to that, indeed, since the latter part of the Roman occupation in the fourth century AD, the Christian church had been gradually displacing the worship of much older Celtic deities. Overt sexual expression was no longer tolerated and intercourse was perceived as a base and sinful act, a gratuitous indulgence in which demanded repentance and absolution. In its place were founded the ideals of romantic – and preferably unconsummated – love. But even a cursory perusal of medieval art and literature uncovers an abundance of erotic references and iconography that would have incurred the wrath of any devout clergyman. So it seems there was a considerable discrepancy between what the church publicly expected of its flock and what people actually got up to.

Many pagan sites had, for thousands of years before the arrival of the Romans, been the focus of rituals performed to ensure the continued fertility of a bountiful Mother Earth. The church sought to sanctify many of these ancient sites, exorcising their pagan associations by the superimposition of Christian symbols or places of worship. The house and gardens of Lord Holles were built on the post-Dissolution site of a Benedictine abbey that had dominated life here for over five hundred years. It is possible that the site of the monastery, founded in AD 987, was originally chosen to Christianise an existing pagan symbol. Suggestions have even been made that it was the monks themselves who carved the figure in jest, when the last abbot, Thomas Corton, was dismissed for alleged depravity and 'malpractice'.

Long before then, the Roman army had brought fundamental change to the society of native Britain. After the invasion of AD 43, most of England was quickly and effectively subdued and existing Celtic culture soon became merged with new ideas from the continent. The phallus was already widespread throughout Roman culture as a symbol of potency and good luck, and this was now prolifically displayed in outdoor settings in the form of carved stones and painted murals. Some parts of Britain, however, never succumbed to attempts by imperial forces to take over, and here the Celtic traditions were strongly maintained. One emperor, Commodus, was rather obsessive about the god Hercules – a club-wielding deity, commonly associated with fertility. In the belief that he was a reincarnation of this classical god, Commodus attempted to revive the practice of Herculean worship and it has been suggested that the Cerne giant was carved during the resurgence of this cult. But Commodus, it seems, never actually set foot in Britain. Scheduled to arrive on the first of January AD 193 to demonstrate his divinity and invincibility, his attendance was prevented by his assassination on the last day of AD 192.

Despite such setbacks, the Roman period saw the first major period of urbanisation in Britain. Although not on the scale of the Industrial Revolution of the nineteenth century, this transition contributed to a process in which native people became gradually estranged from the intimate relationship with the natural landscape that had characterised pre-Roman society.

No archaeological evidence has yet been found to indicate that people in prehistoric Britain lacked awareness of their own sexuality. On the contrary, all the evidence points towards an ability and desire to express sexuality through complex symbolism and metaphor. The problem, in fact, is ours. Trying to understand the subtleties of another culture with twenty-first-century minds means that the decoding of many features must remain open to interpretation. A wealth of material from Europe, Asia and South America does, however, testify to the fact that several thousand years ago there already existed a great variation in human sexual culture. Clues can be found in the form of carvings, pottery and stone figurines to a variety of sexual practices that any one would recognise today, including transvestism, prostitution and homosexuality.

It was just such sexually aware people who, five thousand years ago, felt compelled to leave their tasks of everyday subsistence to construct vast monuments that still dominate landscapes in Britain and Ireland. Great mounds of earth hundreds of metres in length stretch past circles of enormous upright standing stones, the erection of which would test the ability of modern engineers. These structures have no obvious practical purpose but the physical effort invested in building them (without the benefit of modern earth-moving machinery) and the

Buried deep within the Irish passage tomb of Knowth, this carved phallus graphically illustrates the complex connection between the earth, death and sex.

cooperation of labour required to make it possible is staggering.

Often, archaeologists are concerned with understanding the practicalities of daily life but what if, to prehistoric people, daily life meant something other than what we imagine? At some point there developed a belief in animism – the concept that trees and rocks, waterfalls and the wind, all had spirits. The earth was venerated as a great female deity, and the sun was perceived as a powerful male force. These gods and goddesses, intimately connected to the survival of all living things, were worshipped and entreated through ceremony – and even, it seems, appeased by human sacrifice.

Today, we tend to view events from a linear perspective, as phenomena that progress forwards in a straight line. Prehistoric people, however, worked on the principle of cyclicity. For these farmers, intimately connected to their surroundings, the cycles of life and death and of the seasons were of fundamental importance to their survival. Sex was an essential part in this cyclical theatre, a source of pleasure and a means of reproduction. The fertility of the earth was perceived as inseparable from human sexuality. Through sympathetic magic, human copulation in the fields at planting time would encourage the land to fruitfulness and ensure a good harvest –

not to mention one or two new additions to the tribe.

An interpretation and expression of sexuality was a two-way process. In the natural landscape, hills that resembled breasts or a swollen, pregnant belly were acknowledged as the voluptuous body of the earth goddess and caves and underground tunnels were endowed with sacred status befitting the womb of mother earth. But people also reciprocated with their own symbolic creations. Throughout Britain and Ireland, monuments were built either for use in ceremonies focusing on human sexuality or to illustrate the abundance that was desired of the earth.

And it is to the prehistoric period – to the centuries just before the arrival of the Romans in Britain – that the bold chalk figure of the Cerne Abbas Giant is most often attributed. Over one hundred miles further east, another enormous depiction had also been scoured in the tussocky grass.

The Long Man of Wilmington, facing inland from the East Sussex shore on Windover Hill, is second in size only to the Giant of Attacama in Chile. He has been attributed, in the past, to Phoenician traders travelling the high level routes from Cornwall and Wessex and to medieval monks at the Wilmington priory. Similar images have been found on a diminutive scale on an Anglo-Saxon belt buckle from Finglesham in Kent and a rock carving by Lake Onege in northern Russia. The Long Man is not as physically explicit as the giant at Cerne Abbas but he does have what appear to be two tall staffs. No firm conclusion has been reached as to what these represent but it may be relevant that in Scandinavia the Norse god Baldur is depicted in a strikingly similar fashion, holding open the gates of spring. There are even folk tales of a female partner who once adorned the slopes of a nearby hill. So it is possible that the Long Man is one of the biggest fertility symbols in the world. He certainly has come to represent as much in modern times; on the first of May 2002 the figure received an explicit addition. Perhaps in celebration of the Celtic festival of Beltane, a May Day fertility rite, or perhaps just to make him feel less inadequate, a knee-length appendage was painted on the grass between his legs.

We may never know if the original chalk figures were made in the likeness of an Anglo-Saxon god or were the work of a Celtic fertility cult. In many ways, the mystery of their creation adds to their appeal. What matters more is how people have reacted to them in the past and how we continue to react to them today. The figures are both now carefully maintained so that, regardless of their origins, their survival into the future is assured – enabling visitors and locals to connect for a while with part of Britain's rich history of sexual landscapes.

9

The Long Man of Wilmington is one of the largest existing symbols of fertility, holding open the gates of spring.

In researching and photographing *Landscapes and Desire*, we were fortunate to have an opportunity to explore the entire British Isles. We took a fresh look at some familiar places along with many that are virtually unknown. At the outset, our intention was to look only at Britain but inevitably we were drawn to the furthest corners of the British Isles. Part of Ireland and the Channel Islands rendered up sites too sumptuously sexual to ignore; and these have also made their way on to the pages of this book. But whatever the location, we were constantly amazed by what we found. Stunning natural landscapes, from the soft-sided chalky Downs to gnarled and craggy moorland, have been the canvas for five thousand years of cultural influences as diverse as Scandinavian Vikings and Renaissance Italy. We also met some of the fascinating and humorous people who animate this awe-inspiring stage and talked to some who have been inspired to create their own contribution to this outdoor archive of sexual sites.

In 1946, George Mikes wrote, in *How to be an Alien*, 'Continental people have a sex life; the British have hot water bottles.' George Mikes was wrong – Britain is, in fact, a wonderfully rude place.

The following chapters take us on a journey that begins with the earliest prehistoric monuments of desire. Most of the places mentioned – from megalithic temples to tiny medieval carvings – are listed at the end of the book, in the gazetteer which provides readers with sufficient information to find and explore these sites for themselves. This is not intended to be a definitive text book or the last word on the history of licentious landscapes; it is rather a taste of what has gone unnoticed by many people for so long. It is a first step towards re-introducing ourselves to a landscape where desolate stone circles, ravaged by the north wind and haunted by the fluid cry of the curlew, combine effortlessly with outrageous and luxurious stately gardens. The resulting legacy is an environment as beautiful, quirky and intriguing as any on earth.

The stones at Callanish Tursachan are of the subtlest pale hues and lined with delicate filaments of quartz.

CHAPTER TWO

Romancing the Stone

ONE OF THE DEEPEST ABSURDITIES IN OUR CULTURE IS THE
UNACKNOWLEDGEMENT OF SEXUAL SYMBOLISM . . . YET EVERY COUNTRY,
EVERY CULTURE, HAS A GREAT AND COMMON STOCK OF PHALLIC,
TESTICULAR, VULVULAR OR MAMMARY OBJECTS.

ANTHONY WEIR

From the wide waters of the Burry Inlet on the southern coast of Wales, the Gower Peninsula rises to a windy ridge of farmland – and to an ancient pillar of stone known as Samson's Jack or, more bluntly, Samson's Erection. Today the modern road affords few glimpses of the sea, and the stone is entirely hidden from view. But older routes, those forged by the first farmers of this fertile peninsula, stuck to higher ground and up here the dazzling white column of quartz thrusts skyward in a gesture that is timeless. This obelisk stands where it was hauled on end long before Christianity reached these unspoiled shores, a magnificent monument to pagan virility. Samson's Jack is only one of many stone phalluses that survive throughout the countryside of Britain and

Ireland – the remains of what can only be described as a prehistoric penis obsession.

It is tempting to dismiss these solitary standing stones as nothing more than functional markers. After all, many of them are found in remote or upland countryside where signposts may have been needed to inform prehistoric travellers that they were crossing tribal boundaries or following the known route. But these areas of moorland and isolated farms were not necessarily always so marginal. Five thousand years ago, during the period known as the Neolithic – or New Stone Age – the climate was considerably warmer than today. For the first time settlers were able to cultivate slopes high above the sheltered river valleys, so these obelisks may once have stood in the

Samson's Jack – or
Samson's Erection – is a
sparkling pillar of quartz
on the Welsh Gower
peninsula.

heart of small pioneering communities and the landscape which supported them. Like Samson's Jack, stone phalluses often only survive in places spared from the encroaching demands of urban society but must once have been rampant among the fields and hills of the British Isles.

While many of these erections stand alone as solitary statements of virility, others can be found competing for attention in multiple settings of two or more stones. The site of Harold's Stones lies in the Welsh village of Trellech – a name derived from the direct translation of 'three stones'. In lush green pasture, three massive pillars stand on end, each stone beautifully shaped and proportioned and unquestionably phallic. The tallest reaches an impressive height of over four metres above the ground and points at what might be described as an enthusiastic angle. This pillar contains fragments of white and rose quartz which, in sunlight, make the stone sparkle with delicate hues of pinky white. The extra effort required to heave three such columns into place suggests that these were intended to do more than mark a trackway but why would prehistoric people invest so much time and energy in erecting a structure with no apparent purpose? Clues to this have recently been uncovered much further north, across the Scottish border, where some particularly suggestive members of a stone circle have been identified.

The striking silhouette of Harold's Stones at Trellech in Wales – a multiple setting of phallic pillars.

It would be easy to pass near Aikey Brae without being aware of its presence. There is no sign from the road that it exists and a dense coniferous woodland completely shrouds the stones from view. The merest trace of a path, formed of fist-sized rocks nestled in the carpet of pine needles, marks a way through to the other side of the forest, and is the first hint that your presence is expected. This is the stuff of fairy tales and a gingerbread cottage would not seem out of place here. Emerging from the shadows into a brilliantly sunlit clearing it takes a moment to take in this delightfully rude display of laddish prowess.

One of the circle stones at Aikey Brae in Aberdeenshire displays a fine attention to anatomical detail.

One of the stones, a majestic arcing column, is festooned with moss and lichen of myriad shades of green from silvery sage to almost black. At its tip, nature, perhaps with a sense of humour, has added a slender eyelet-shaped hollow. The glans of another is meticulously defined by a delicate stony ridge. By their very nature, pillars of stone placed vertically are prone to being somewhat phallic in appearance but even the most sceptical onlooker would have to admit that some of those at Aikey Brae show a surprising attention to anatomical detail. While there is no sign of artificial sculpting or carving it seems impossible that the builders of this circle were unaware of the stones' overtly sexual appearance. It is equally unlikely that their inclusion is purely serendipitous. Instead, it seems the stones were carefully selected for their naturally suggestive shapes and brought to this inspiring hilltop where they were erected in a ring of great sexual significance.

Aikey Brae belongs to a distinctive group of prehistoric monuments known as recumbent stone circles. Found in an area of north-east Scotland that correlates roughly to modern Aberdeenshire, the name is derived from a single horizontal, or recumbent, stone always present like a gigantic altar in the rings of otherwise upright stones. This level slab, invariably in the southern quadrant of the circle, is flanked by two pillars in a pattern that is repeated throughout the region.

The recumbent circle of Whitehill near Tillyfourie lies north of a breath-taking expanse of land with sweeping views to the south and hills beyond. But this circle has not endured the five thousand years since its creation unscathed. A hefty recumbent of grey stone, veined delicately with lacy white quartz, lies immovable, but many of the pillars surrounding it have succumbed to gravity and toppled among the bracken. Only one flanking stone, that to the west of the recumbent, is still standing. This comically phallic upright is fabulously ridged. It turns visitors into voyeurs and cannot fail to convince that whoever erected the recumbent circle of Whitehill not only knew exactly what they wanted to achieve, but also that they had a sense of humour.

The flanker to the east is one of the casualties of time. A broad, flat slab, now prostrate where it fell, this stone's appearance could not contrast more sharply with the phallic column to the west. The different shapes of the stones seem so marked as to be deliberate but is it possible that prehistoric circle-builders were also employing a form of opposite sexuality – female as well as male symbolism – in the stones?

To the north-west of Aberdeen is a Late Neolithic stone circle known as Loanhead of Daviot. Here, a

A majestic arcing column at Aikey Brae, festooned with moss and lichen, and with a slender eyelet-shaped hollow at its tip.

The horizontal stone and flanking male pillar still survive at the recumbent stone circle of Whitehill in Aberdeenshire.

level platform was cut into the hillside to accommodate this ring of ten upright stones and a recumbent block, shattered by prehistoric ice into two thin slabs of stone. As at Whitehill, one of the flankers, though not of great stature, is a beautifully defined petrified phallus. Again, its partner on the other side of the recumbent is a much broader slab of stone. This raises questions about the sexual depiction being used since clearly this is not a literal portrayal of female genitalia. Instead it seems that the builders of these circles were employing a recognised abstract symbol to represent the concept of female.

Artists had been busy elsewhere within the Loanhead circle. The inner face of another pillar was carved with twelve small depressions or 'cup marks'. Cut from the rock in a vertical line, the hollows make this pillar stand out as significant among the others and the reason lies in the orientation of the stone from the centre of the circle. Carefully positioned at 139 degrees from north, on the darkest day in the year the midwinter sun appears to brush the side of this stone as it rises. This unusual phenomenon may suggest a connection between the exceptionally phallic nature of the western flanker and this circle's orientation towards what was regarded as the male energy of the renewing solstice sun.

In 1932 the site was excavated, with some surprising results. Each of the pillars had been erected, not on fresh ground, but over a small, cairn-covered pit containing carefully deposited charcoal and pieces of broken pottery. This was not discarded waste but a collection of objects that had been ritually broken or 'killed' then placed within the earth to imbue this site with specific meaning. Far from being simple prehistoric pornography these stones, it seems, formed powerful places whose underlying theme was connected to sexuality.

A few miles south of the village of Insch stands a conifer plantation where the pines are widely enough spaced that sunlight penetrates on to a verdant carpet

Opposite Whitehill's recumbent stone, a tiny phallic post rises above the bracken.

Cothiemuir Wood in Aberdeenshire is one of Scotland's finest recumbent circles, the stones of which display classic male and female shaping.

of knee-deep grass that still sparkles at midday with drenching dew. Here, within the barcode of vertical tree trunks, a rebel diagonal form catches the eye – the magnificent triangular female stone of the Cothiemuir Wood Circle. Both the flanking stones are of beautiful red granite but from one side this upright almost has the appearance of a heavy-breasted woman. It contrasts markedly with the chisel-straight column to the east of the recumbent but both are clearly abstract depictions of male and female sexuality. Like all recumbent circles, the stones are graded in height from the towering flankers to a diminutive pillar directly opposite. At Cothiemuir, however, the appearance of this smallest member is overtly phallic, defining this stone as an important element of the circle.

At over four metres in length and weighing twenty tonnes, the recumbent stone lies in the grass like a deflating beached whale, its dark basalt hide speckled with pale lichen. Faint cup-marks, known as the Devil's Hoofmarks, which can be discerned on its outer side may indicate that here, too, we should look to the skies for a celestial connection. From the smallest stone opposite, the enormous recumbent is aligned on the path of the major southern moonset. That ceremonies took place at Cothiemuir Wood is suggested by the discovery of burnt deposits buried beneath a ring cairn in the centre of the circle –

perhaps these took place by moonlight when a lunar glow reflected on the grey flanks of the massive horizontal stone. The footprints of those who performed their rites here have long since faded, but by looking again at what these sites have in common we may come a little closer to understanding what the builders of this circle were striving for.

The location of recumbent circles was of fundamental importance to their prehistoric architects. Prominent positions were chosen with clear views to the south, indeed the stones' alignment suggests that the observation of the major southern moon was focal to their design. The stones around the circle decrease in height towards the setting moon then rise again, in imitation, maybe, of its waxing and waning. Crystals of brilliant white quartz found scattered within the circle interiors would have gleamed under a full moon and were perhaps intended to represent its milky light. All this becomes immediately poignant when we consider that the moon was anciently associated with the cycles of birth, menstruation and regeneration.

Areas of rich earth have been found near this and many other recumbent circles, giving rise to a theory that soil was brought to the site to symbolise what was being sought. Offerings of ritually broken items and possibly even human sacrifice were deposited beside the beautifully contrasting male and female

stones. These were ceremonial places where deities were invoked through the moon – perhaps even through ritual copulation – and where human sexuality was perceived as inextricably connected to the fertility of the land.

The recumbent circles of Aberdeenshire are certainly intriguing monuments but they constitute only part of the British Isles' rich heritage of sexually inspired sites. For two thousand years, until the Middle Bronze Age (around 1200 BC), Britain and Ireland were gripped by megalithic mania. Standing stones and circles were erected from the Irish seaboard as far as the Northern Isles in Scotland and Cornwall in the south and regional variations soon began to appear. Not all circles were formed of gigantic pillars; many included quite diminutive boulders and while some rings were beautiful in their simplicity others were impressively complex. But the subtle interplay between Britain's early farmers, their untamed landscape and the stones they erected within it is perhaps nowhere more eloquently expressed than on the rugged isle of Arran off Scotland's west coast.

The location of Machrie Moor, on a broad peaty terrace high above the stormy grey waters of Kilbrannan Sound, could hardly be more stunning. The valley of Machrie Glen leads to the north-east where clouds constantly boil and swirl over the dark peak of the evocatively named mountain of Garbh

In a pattern repeated throughout the recumbent circles of Scotland, the smallest stone at Cothiemuir Wood is a diminutive phallus.

On Machrie Moor on the island of Arran a spectacular array of red male sandstone columns tower above the peaty floor.

Thorr like some Shakespearean hag's cauldron. A long ridge of hills stretches down to the east, including Ard Bheinn, whose name is reminiscent of Ard, or Urd – the Scandinavian mother goddess. The very name Machrie is an ancient reference to the fertility of this level plain where people lived and farmed six thousand years ago. And on this small area of sacred ground they built an arena for direct communion with the gods which has come to be described as the most impressive group of architecturally diverse circles in western Europe.

Three gigantic sandstone slabs dominate the moor, where ochre columns rising out of the peat to a height of over five metres are set in an arc that was once part of a complete circle. One of them pierces the ground, a stylised lightning bolt, and the tops of all three have been fluted by erosion into monolithic quivers of arrows. The fate of the missing stones is betrayed by two large fragments lying amongst the reeds. During the Industrial Revolution attempts were made to turn these majestic uprights into millstones, but perhaps the task of moving them proved too daunting and the broken, partly-worked carcasses were abandoned where they lie today. To the west stands the solitary survivor of another decimated circle where the remains of a man in his early twenties were recovered from the peat. The burial here of an individual in the prime of virility may have

Suidhe Choir Fhionn or Fingal's Cauldron Seat has become woven into Scottish mythology but its prehistoric creators were representing female sexuality in the low granite boulders.

held significance in this ring of towering 'male' columns, but it was not only masculinity that found expression on Machrie Moor.

On a ridge of higher ground, with sweeping views across the moor, is a double concentric ring of boulders. Fourteen low, bulbous lumps of granite surround an inner circle of eight white quartz boulders known as Suidhe Choir Fhionn or Fingal's Cauldron Seat. Local legend maintains that the heroic giant Fingal used to cook within the ring, tying his dog Bran to a nearby holed stone. But their design, it seems, was not originally intended to fulfil any practical purpose, and these stones have instead been interpreted as symbolic of the female element of the group. A similar meaning has been suggested for a compact setting of four low granite boulders below Suidhe Choir Fhionn. Although probably incomplete, it is possible to discern a slight grading in height with the lowest circle stone aligned to the south-west – the direction of the setting sun on the darkest day of midwinter.

The final ring to be explored in the Machrie Moor group is a wonderful blend of symbolically male and female stones. Six 'female' boulders of grey biotite granite, barely knee-high and brought to Machrie Glen from the north of the island by Ice Age glaciers, are set in a perfect ellipse. These stones have been alternately set with small slabs of red microgranite found locally near the moor – miniature versions of

soaring monoliths barely thirty centimetres in height. These early circles, it seems, were built by people using not only different shapes but an intimate knowledge of geological variations in a sophisticated language of sexual symbolism.

For a long time archaeologists have been puzzled by the fact that, in the vastness of Machrie Moor, all the circles are concentrated in one small area. The reason for this became apparent when it was recently proved that when the midsummer sun rises over the mountainous horizon, this is the only place on the whole moor where the first brilliant flash of light coincides with a notch in the skyline at the head of the glen. From the grading of the female boulders it is clear that the circles' architects were aware of this solar path. Viewed from the sexually-charged stones, the sun's appearance at a marked point in the landscape on an auspicious morning during the year must have been a high point in the calendar of Arran's early inhabitants.

In too many instances to be coincidental, ancient stones like those of Glenquickan in Dumfries were built in elevated, naturally dramatic locations. Clearly, the landscape formed an interactive backdrop to these open-air stages where worshippers in prehistoric fertility cults would gather to witness the penetrating rays of dawn and to entreat a fruitful union between the male energy of the Sun and the

Glenquickan stone circle occupies an exposed moorland in Dumfries — an elegant combination of 'female' boulders and a central bulbous phallus.

Mother Earth. But such sites are by no means unique to Scotland; the English Lake District is home to one of the earliest – and most spectacularly sited – stone circles in Europe.

Castlerigg surmounts a high, rounded knoll that stands like an elevated stage surrounded by a natural amphitheatre of formidable mountains. Until recent times, bonfires were lit here in celebration of the Celtic fertility festival of Samhain, and for centuries this ancient site has provided inspiration for writers and poets. Keats imagined it to be a 'Druid temple' although by the time these spiritual leaders rose to power the stones of Castlerigg had already been standing for three thousand years.

The Sanctuary at Castlerigg in Cumbria houses the circle's tallest pillar of stone, oriented towards St John's Beck and to the sunrise on the Celtic festival of Samhain.

Two green-grey pillars flank the entrance of this circle of local slate. From here the gaze is drawn towards the valley of St John's Beck – the only break in an enfolding ring of hills. In line with the valley stands a rectangular group of stones known as the Sanctuary. It includes the tallest pillar at Castlerigg, at the base of which a deep pit was uncovered during excavations in 1882. The pit, which was filled with a mixture of charcoal and rich earth, was a ritual deposit created as the result of two deliberate acts. The first involved penetrating the soil, life-supporter of these superstitious people, followed by placing a fertile offering within the earth to encourage it to fruitfulness. This tallest pillar and its ceremonial pit align precisely with a point in the valley to the south-east where the sun rises on the first day of November – or Samhain.

An arena of stones was erected in this fortuitous place where the profile of the horizon combined with the cycles of the sun to create a theatrical backdrop on a monumental scale. Chanting, feasting, even ritual copulation, would have combined in the dramas conducted against this scene of nature at its most awesome. Performed on specific days within the calendar such acts would have been imbued with exceptional meaning for these early farmers wishing to ensure the fertility of their crops and animals. Castlerigg provided its prehistoric architects with a focus for their attempts to influence the forces of nature that affected both their lives and their surroundings. But just as standing stones and the component pillars of circles were often invested with sexual power, so too was sexuality sometimes recognised in the land itself. To prehistoric people the earth was seen as a female entity, a nurturing mother who could give – and also withhold – the resources so essential to survival.

On the Outer Hebridean island of Lewis the silhouetted outline of a female recumbent figure can be seen in the mountains of the west coast. Named Cailleach na Mòintich, the Old Woman of the Moors,

The hoary phallus of Cnoc Fillibhear Bheag is one of the most suggestive standing stones in the British Isles. It is said to court a trinity of Celtic goddesses embodied within the stones of the circle.

27

The phallic stone at Cnoc Fillibhear Bheag aligns with the rounded headland and a gap in the distant hills.

she was recognised, even revered, by the earliest inhabitants of the island. The landscape in her shadow is bursting with prehistoric ceremonial sites, and one of the most intriguing stands on a headland above the waters of Loch Roag, where the light has a rare clarity and the the curlew can be heard high overhead.

Cnoc Fillibhear Bheag is a fine double ellipse originally of thirteen uprights – most of which still stand rooted to the ground from which they were hewn. Three stones of the inner ellipse have been interpreted as the ancient Earth Goddess in her trinity of forms as Maiden, Mother and Crone and each is courted by a single jagged, lichen-covered phallus. But despite the primeval beauty of these stones the eyes are lured beyond the circle to a breath-taking panorama across the sparkling loch and the distant dark blue hills. The foreground rises like a swollen pregnant belly beyond which two hills on the far horizon, the open knees of Mother Earth, are separated by a gaping cleft. Ancient people were handed a superbly suggestive backdrop at Cnoc Fillibhear Bheag and they responded by erecting a very phallic stone here, thrusting out of the peat to fill the space between the hills.

Less than a mile away, and also under the omnipresent gaze of Cailleach na Mòintich, is the site of Callanish Tursachan – a stone circle of perhaps incomparable beauty. As another dawn strikes silently from the east the stones glow orange against an uncertain purple sky. It is impossible to resist touching these radiant pillars with fingers tracing their delicately veined and laminated surface, and to do so is to connect briefly with rock formed three billion years ago.

Five thousand years ago this soil was tilled by pioneering farmers, but something interrupted this agricultural scene. The fields were left unploughed, heather began to cover the places where crops once grew and, instead of cultivating food here, the people now hauled giant stones to this lofty rise.

In the first phase of construction at Callanish Tursachan a mighty central pillar of Lewissian gneiss was erected on the ridge. Perhaps in a bid to appease an angered goddess or to return fertility to the female earth this enormous stone phallus, almost five metres in height, was erected high above the loch. Long after this gigantic symbol of virility had been erected the female element was added, an elliptical ring widely used throughout the Outer Hebrides. Of the subtlest pale hues, these stones are lined with delicate filaments of quartz. An imposing avenue of tall thin stones like the aisle of an open-air cathedral stretches towards the exact point on the northern horizon at which the major southern moon sets.

Further astronomical alignments can be witnessed here. Three short rows of stones extend to the east, south and west creating what looks from the air uncannily like a Celtic cross. One row points east towards the beautiful constellation of the Pleiades while in the opposite direction the stones are precisely oriented on the equinoctial sunsets. Incredibly, Callanish Tursachan came to the attention of an ancient Greek historian, Diodorus Siculus, after it had already been abandoned for nine hundred years. He described the 'spherical temple' where the moon 'dances continuously the night through from the vernal equinox until the rising of the Pleiades'. But impressive as this temple's celestial positioning may

Midsummer dawn at Callanish Tursachan where the 'Callanish Phallus' was 'placed thrustfully erect in the middle of a ring dedicated to rituals of sex' – A. Burl.

be, it is its location on the ground that offers clues to the reason for its construction.

To people who regarded the earth as a female deity the evident earthy face, breasts and body of the recumbent Cailleach na Mòintich would have given special meaning to the headland where they built a temple to fertility. The stone phallus and the solar alignments together with the circle and its lunar connections were interwoven to form an intricate plea to the Mother Earth to replenish their harvests.

As recently as the nineteenth century, the fecund powers of the circle were acknowledged by the people of Lewis. Betrothal vows made at Callanish were binding and the stones were considered an auspicious place to consummate a marriage. Attendance at these stones for the ancient festivals of May Day and midsummer morning is a tradition that stretches back to a time before Christianity reached the shores of Lewis – and one that the present-day Church in this remote part of Scotland still strongly disapproves of.

In the Late Neolithic and Early Bronze Ages sexual alliances between individuals may well have been an important tool in forging and maintaining political bonds between neighbouring tribes. Seeking a partner – or several – beyond the immediate clan also strengthened a group's chances of survival by the introduction of diverse genes, and although there was no knowledge of genetic function it is possible that the desire to avoid inbreeding was an instinctive one.

Prehistoric villages have been discovered throughout the Northern Isles at places like Skara Brae on the island of Orkney, which was first exposed in 1850 when the Bay of Skaill was pounded by a great storm. But these are isolated settlements often with no more than ten or so homes suggesting that the population of a much wider area would, on occasion, have gathered together to exchange goods, news and perhaps to find a mate.

On the Orkney mainland a narrow land bridge separates the waters of the Loch of Stenness and the Loch of Harray and this is the site of a daunting circle-henge known as the Ring of Brodgar. Gigantic but thin slabs of Orcadian sandstone rise out of the dark brown heather in a vast circle of standing stones 103 metres in diameter – the third largest in the British Isles. A wide, deep ditch cut into solid rock surrounds the stones, breached in two places by causewayed entrances to the circle. Now peaty and waterlogged, the ditch is clearly defined by a swathe of dancing, white-tufted cotton-grass and everywhere delicate purple orchids shelter from the wind among the rough, dark heather.

Very little is known about this desolate and enigmatic place. Even the age of the circle has never

Tufts of cotton-grass at Orkney's Ring of Brodgar.

A swathe of cotton-grass defines the ditch encircling Orkney's Ring of Brodgar.

been ascertained but a ritual purpose to the stones was recognised as long ago as 1694. On a visit to Orkney, James Garden observed that the Ring of Brodgar and the nearby Standing Stones of Stenness together were 'reputed to be high places of worship and sacrifice in Pagan times . . . the ancient Temples of the Gods'. While no evidence has yet been found to suggest that anyone was ever ritually dispatched among these stones, this was certainly a major ceremonial centre in the prehistoric Northern Isles.

Winter here is a time of long darkness hours, the sun in late December barely climbing above the horizon. We cannot overestimate the importance to these early farmers of the solstice turning point when light, warmth and a hope of regeneration returned. To the south-east of the circle is an outlying monolith known as the Comet Stone. Much squatter than the elegant circle stones, at just 1.8 metres in height, this stone was placed in exact alignment with the midwinter sunrise, an orientation that was probably fundamental to the ceremonial function of the circle. It may also be significant that a stone axe was found within the circle – an object elsewhere associated with the fertility cult worship of the sun.

The Brodgar circle is formed of two quite distinctive shapes of standing stone. Straight, narrow pillars contrast starkly with wide waisted lozenges or triangles and these are thought to be the most highly stylised depiction of the male and female shapes seen elsewhere. Able to accommodate over one thousand people, the full capacity of this site would have been required only for special events in the calendars of the islands' prehistoric inhabitants. As early as 1851 the antiquarian F.W.L. Thomas pondered the 'ante-nuptial ceremonies performed therein' that could explain the function of the Brodgar stones.

This use of sexual symbols was not restricted to the Northern Isles; indeed, identically-shaped stones have been found in Wales and as far south as Cornwall. On the south side of Bodmin Moor, in a landscape that still bears the scars of the long-abandoned Cornish mining industry, is a ceremonial complex known as the Hurlers. Here the remains of three magnificent stone circles stand in line, defiant against the effects of time. The interior of the middle circle was strewn with glimmering sherds – the result of hammer-dressing these pillars of local granite, and evidence that some of them have been artificially shaped. These male and female stones are not as grand in stature as those of Brodgar but their widespread occurrence suggests that they constituted an abstract language the meaning of which was of such fundamental importance to society that it was understood throughout the prehistoric British Isles. And one has to admire the handiwork – or maybe the humour – of those ancient stone masons. As if to emphasise the sexual nature of the stones, in the south-east of the central ring, they included a pillar of outrageously phallic appearance.

William Stukeley was intrigued by the fact that many of Britain's prehistoric circles were often associated with a consummated union of the sexes. He cited the example of Stanton Drew in Somerset, alternatively known as the Weddings, but noted that there were numerous examples of folklore and place names attesting to a long-held connection between stone circles and bawdy celebration. The Nine Maidens in Cornwall were, according to legend, a party of impious girls turned to stone for dancing on the Sabbath. The Merry Maidens suffered a similar fate along with their Pipers. The account by Celia Fiennes of her travels through Cumbria in 1698

Lozenge-shaped stones at the Ring of Brodgar have been interpreted as abstract female depictions.

Withstanding extreme weathering, the exposed columns at Brodgar's stone circle on Orkney are symbols of male sexuality.

explains that the pillars known as Long Meg and her Daughters were actually sisters: 'the story is that those soliciting her unto an unlawful love by an enchantment are turned with her to stone'. The list is long and it points to a reputation founded in more than pure coincidence.

The power of oral history should not be underestimated. Legends that surround such stones are rooted in a genuine cultural memory of debauched behaviour at these sites, passed on through generations by word of mouth. Petrifaction, dispensed as punishment for wicked and impious

Three stone circles known as the Hurlers stood on Bodmin moor in Cornwall long before the landscape was pock-marked by the tin mining industry.

acts, is typical of propaganda spread by an early Christian church intent on deterring scenes of revelry among its flock – especially on a Sunday. Today such legends survive as folklore clues to the pagan origins of these sites as venues for sexually related activities.

The indomitable arches of Stonehenge in Wiltshire have earned this site a place among the wonders of the ancient world. Stonehenge rises from a wide grassy plain that is dense with the remains of Neolithic and Bronze Age monuments. In this sacred landscape of temples and burial mounds, everyday activities were

35

The inclusion of such an outrageously phallic stone in the central Hurlers circle was a deliberate and symbolic act.

forbidden. Described as the most 'skilful combination of engineering, astronomy and symbolism', Stonehenge is unquestionably a triumph of engineering and the plausible astronomical alignments seem endless. But it is the last element – the symbolism locked within these stones – that gives us the real clues as to what Stonehenge is fundamentally about.

The famous site, with its ring of sarsens conjoined by lintels and its massive trilithons so synonymous with British archaeology, was actually built in several phases by as many as seventy-five generations of people. Begun just before 3000 BC, the first version comprised a spacious but simple earthwork henge – a round ditch and inner bank over one hundred metres in diameter. From the details of the layout it is evident that the builders of this early monument were fully aware of the subtly changing pattern of the moon's path across the sky. The main entrance to the north-east was oriented on the most northerly rising of the midwinter full moon, an alignment that would have taken at least two generations to observe accurately. A single outlying stone known as the Heel Stone was erected and this, too, lay in line with a significant lunar point on the horizon. Lastly, fifty-six pits known today as the Aubrey Holes were added inside the bank, again in positions that reflected the movements of the moon. In many cultures moon worship is associated with a female deity, no doubt partly because of the link between lunar and menstrual cycles. When freshly dug from the chalky ground, the ditch would have gleamed – a circle of brilliant white. Was this also symbolic of the moon, made more poignant by its being carved from the very body of the Earth Goddess?

It was not until around 2200 BC that the first bluestones were brought to Stonehenge. From Carn Meini in the Preseli Mountains of south-west Wales, they were carried to within seven miles of Stonehenge by glacially associated activity. These pillars of diorite and rhyolite, which, true to their name, acquire a blueish hue when wet, were set up in two concentric rings. Most importantly, the whole axis of the circle was rotated through four degrees by widening the entrance and creating the illusion that the Heel Stone lay almost in line with the midsummer sunrise. An avenue formed of earthen banks, and probably a processional approach route, extended for a quarter of a mile to the north-east.

In the eighteenth century William Stukeley suspected that there was a solar connection at Stonehenge. This change in angle towards a solar alignment may explain the Heel Stone's name – from the Celtic *freos heol* meaning 'ascending sun'. It certainly heralded a shift in awareness from the moon to the sun – more usually associated with a male sky god. At this time the four Station Stones were set up in a precise rectangle outside the bluestones and they hold the answer to Stonehenge's specific location. Crucially, Stonehenge lies on the precise latitude where both the sunrise and moonrise at midsummer and midwinter are at ninety degrees to one another. The gentle moon, it seems, was not entirely forsaken in favour of this dazzling new deity.

By 2000 BC the bluestone circles had been dismantled and work began on the design so familiar today. Huge sandstone sarsens were dragged eighteen miles from the Marlborough Downs and erected in a horseshoe. Five enormous settings, each of two uprights joined by a horizontal stone – a trilithon – towered in increasing height towards the south-west and the midwinter sunset. In some cultures the trilithon, like a gigantic doorway, symbolises the vagina – an entrance to the womb of Mother Earth. Around these stood a perfect circle of sarsens almost thirty metres in diameter. Not only were these stones fitted together with millimetre accuracy but they were also skilfully tapered towards the top, creating an illusion of even greater height. Incredibly, despite the ground's slope down towards the River Avon, the ring of conjoining lintels – each weighing an average of twenty-six tonnes – is perfectly horizontal.

Many cultures of the world regard the trilithon as a symbolic vagina.

Two more stones were also added. Known today as the Slaughter Stone, a recumbent slab near the northern entrance is stained a vivid red not from the blood of sacrificial victims but from iron deposits in the stone. And at the core of the entire monument stood the Altar Stone, a fabulous pillar of Welsh sandstone containing fragments of garnet, imported from what is now Milford Haven in Wales. The stage was set for annual theatricals on a megalithic scale.

Every year at dawn on the midsummer solstice, as the sun showed above the horizon, a shaft of light, framed by the Slaughter Stone, burst in through the vaginal entrance to strike the Altar Stone. Surrounded by its protective uterus of trilithons, this bejewelled stone would have sparkled in the intense first rays of dawn as the Earth Goddess was graphically penetrated by the Sun God. Moments later the phallic shadow of the Heel Stone would have thrust along the same line into the womb of trilithons in a second symbolic penetration, a darker re-enactment of the initial consummation of the gods.

But this was more than abstract drama. To these people the mating of the gods would have been essential to ensuring the continued fecundity of the earth and the fertility of their crops and animals. It took place at a time of year when food was plentiful and the days were long. Small tribal groups, having spent much of the year apart, would have gathered at midsummer to exchange news, barter livestock and tools and ensure the success of the next year's harvest. The consummation of the gods may even have been encouraged and emulated by ceremonial human copulation.

As cars rush over the rounded crest of Overton Hill in Wiltshire, passengers are probably unaware that they are passing within just a few metres of an ancient site which many archaeologists believe was a centre for celebrating the rite of passage into sexual maturity.

Many societies mark this transitional time in life when the sexes are often isolated for a period of instruction or initiation that culminates in a re-entry into society signifying rebirth as a mature adult. It is possible that the Sanctuary was a kind of maze, a symbol often associated with maidenhood.

Modern concrete plinths, set in a series of concentric rings and half buried in the grass, now mark where the Sanctuary once stood, commanding incredible views of the surrounding countryside. Destroyed in the early eighteenth century and actually lost until its rediscovery in the 1930s, the Sanctuary was originally an impressive structure of timber posts open to the sky. A mass of wooden pillars, perhaps carved or brightly painted, these were put up and later removed in a complex series of structural adjustments.

This enigmatic place has not surrendered many secrets to modern inquiry but pits filled with the remains of ceremonial feasting have been found, adding detail to the picture of the great celebrations being held on this hill. At some stage the timber posts were replaced by two concentric stone circles. Against the eastern stone of the inner circle the remains of an adolescent girl were found, buried before the stone was erected. Placed in line with the equinoctial sunrises with a Beaker pot and some animal bones, it seems she was placed here as a sacrifice. This girl was one of many people whose remains were found within the sacred confines of the Sanctuary, and whose presence may have strengthened the connection between the people and their land. The dead dwelt beneath ground and it was from within the earth that all fertility came.

From the Sanctuary on Overton Hill, a stone-lined route extends northward for nearly one and a half miles to the great stone circle and earthwork henge at Avebury. One hundred pairs of stones originally lined this West Kennet Avenue, the tallest reaching over four metres in height, in what has been interpreted as a monumental display of sexual symbolism. Each side of the avenue comprises alternating tall, thin, flat-topped columns and broad-hipped peaked lozenges arranged in pairs of opposite stones that echo a similar pattern seen in stone rows elsewhere in Britain, Ireland and France. Built in stages, each section was sanctified upon completion, with a ritual deposit of beautifully worked flint, pottery – and even human sacrifice. A second, similar route once extended toward the Avebury circle from the west. Known as the Beckhampton Avenue the only stones of this to survive are a pair of gigantic blocks, known as Adam and Eve, that today stand

The tall, thin columns of the West Kennet Avenue mirror patterns seen elsewhere in Britain, Ireland and France.

'Female' broad-hipped stones alternate with 'male' stones in a monumental display of sexual symbolism at Avebury's West Kennet Avenue.

isolated in a field of wheat three-quarters of a mile west of the great circle.

The sinuous route defined by the West Kennet Avenue inspired William Stukeley to suggest that the avenue 'imitated the figure of a snake as drawn in the ancient hieroglyphics'. Perhaps because of its habit of shedding its skin, the snake has been seen as a divine animal and used to represent the cycle of renewal and rebirth. The continuation of life through copulation was embodied in its form and the serpent was embraced as a beneficent force of fertility and growth.

As the West Kennet Avenue approaches the southern, and most spectacular, entrance of the circle the ground rises and the avenue kinks in a design that was intended to keep the interior of the great Avebury circle hidden from view until the last moment. Seeing for the first time the massive ditch and hulking tonnage of stone that is the Avebury circle is an experience never forgotten.

Nearly one hundred stones or 'sarsens', some weighing as much as sixty tonnes, were dragged to Avebury from the slopes of the Marlborough Downs over four thousand years ago. Here the stones were heaved upright into a ring of such colossal dimensions that today two roads and an entire village are bounded within its circumference. Avebury is the biggest prehistoric henge and stone circle in Britain

An undulating outer bank encloses the henge circle of Avebury, screening the interior ceremonial space from view.

and this gargantuan megalithic arena lay at the heart of what, many archaeologists believe, was a ritual landscape built over many years and dedicated to the worship of fertility.

The Avebury stones were never artificially shaped like those at Stonehenge but were chosen for their specific natural shapes, representing male and female sexuality. These were carefully placed with reference to both the major equinoctial sun- and moonrises. A vast ditch was dug encircling the stones, a quarter of a mile in diameter and deep enough to conceal a house. The spoil from this ditch was heaped around the outer edge forming an uneven bank so high it completely obscured the surrounding horizon. This incredible architectural feat was undertaken using the most basic of hand tools: deer antler picks and ox-blade shovels. To complete the work would have taken an estimated one and a half million work hours – a massive investment of labour for these early farmers. But for all this effort the structure did not provide shelter for a single person; even normal, everyday activities, it seems, were taboo in this sacred place.

The circle is a design that appears throughout diverse cultures of the world. A line with neither beginning nor end, the circle echoes the natural cycles of renewal, of seasons, birth, sex and death. It is an ancient symbol intimately associated with fertility and the eternal forces of life. When the ditch at Avebury was first dug into the chalk it would have formed a brilliant white circle. Inside this stood the gigantic monoliths, each block of gnarled grey stone an awesome presence in the ring that formed a massive version of this recognised symbol.

Within the main Avebury circle archaeologists have found traces of two smaller circles, each in themselves of considerable size, whose male and female properties are unmistakable. Within the northernmost circle stood a hollow structure known as the Cove. Originally a three-sided chamber, only two enormous stones remain but these are the most striking in the whole Avebury complex. The Cove was aligned on the point where the most northerly moonrise appears over Hackpen Hill at midwinter, and was romantically named the Luna Circle by William Stukeley.

The southern circle surrounded a single pillar of stone, the tallest at Avebury, known as the Obelisk. In its shadow was a series of deep pits dug into the ground to receive offerings, and filled with the same mixture of rich, black, fertile earth. Although this great phallic monument is no longer standing, its location is marked by a concrete plinth. A clue to its original purpose may be gleaned from accounts that until the nineteenth century, a maypole – the traditional folk representation of the phallus itself – was being erected there.

In addition to interpreting the visible remains, archaeologists have been able to glean information about the Avebury site from excavations. A number of stone axe-heads were discovered, dating from a late Neolithic period when the trade in stone axes was flourishing in Britain. These items were prized possessions whose role was often more ritual than practical. Possibly connected with a sun cult or sky god, the Avebury axes appear not to have been discarded but reverently buried in offering to a highly venerated deity.

One aspect of worship undertaken at Avebury was rather more gruesome than we might expect. When the main henge ditch was excavated in 1908 it was found, incredibly, to descend nine metres deep. The debris and accumulated silt contained the deposits of charcoal, pottery and animal bone usually associated with ritual sites but among these were some surprising finds. Human skulls and long bones discovered here and in the avenue had evidently been separated from their bodies. In one case the long bones had been inserted through the jaw of the skull. The bones of the dead, it appeared, were not laid to rest but taken to the stone circle for use in the ritual activities. It is possible that in a macabre display of deathly theatre the skulls and thighbones were used in a symbolic enactment of sexual penetration.

So Avebury presents us with a landscape of interlinked component sites: the Sanctuary, the avenues and the great henge circle itself. Each one was apparently connected to rituals of a sexual nature but is there any way of knowing how the landscape functioned as a whole? We can be certain that the avenue formed a processional route, in fact archaeologists have discerned that people walked along the outside of the stones rather than between them as we might expect. It is thought that both avenues led to, rather than away from, the main circle, suggesting that two lines of people were converging on the ring of stones. The West Kennet Avenue provided a route from the Sanctuary – a structure that is thought to be linked to rites of sexual maturity in young women. Although we have no way of being certain, it seems possible that the destroyed Beckhampton Avenue was a route taken by young men of the society making the transition from adolescence to maturity. But what happened when these two processional lines reached the main circle.

The sinuous line of the avenue stones, the circle's obscuring bank and imposing entrances were all carefully orchestrated to create an atmosphere of anticipation. Once inside the main circle, the lines of young men and women were presented with the Obelisk and the Cove – two powerful symbols of male and female sexuality. These inner circles clearly

Men-an-Tol in Cornwall is one of the many holed stones throughout the British Isles that are traditionally connected to sexual penetration and even to bonds of marriage.

defined a special place and perhaps only an elite few were allowed inside, the majority being excluded beyond the bank.

In constructing the great stone circle at Avebury the inhabitants of the Marlborough Downs were doing far more than emulating the cycles of reproduction they saw in nature. The architecture of the ring and the ceremonies carried out within were essential components in a vast open-air theatre. We have no way of knowing exactly what took place within the

The moon and stone circles have long been associated with female fertility.

stones, but the repeated re-enactment of sexually imbued rituals was designed to encourage the continued fertility of their tribe and everything upon which it depended.

A single stone once stood at Avebury between the south inner circle and the adjacent entrance. This sarsen had a natural perforation at its top corner which William Stukeley described in 1724 when he wrote 'an odd stone standing, not of great bulk. It has a hole wrought in it, and probably was design'd to fasten the victim, in order for slaying it. This I call the ring-stone'. Now reduced to a shattered stump, it is still referred to as the Ring Stone and although once an important pillar aligned upon the north and south ring centres, it is unlikely ever to have been used to tether sacrificial virgins.

Holed stones occur widely throughout Britain and Ireland and the customs surrounding them have endured tenaciously. Almost always they appear near stone circles or paired with standing stones presenting an undeniably graphic symbol of procreation. Holed stones are also found in association with burials, where it is thought that the bones of ancestors were passed through the hole in a ritual enactment of rebirth.

Until recently, the role of perforated stones seems to have been twofold. For centuries these were used in rites of fertility and healing but, perhaps because of the energy believed to be stored within them, these

pillars also provided a traditional setting for the pledging of vows between young couples.

Men-an-Tol, near the south-westerly tip of Cornwall, lies high on bracken-covered moors. This remarkable setting of stones comprises two uprights and a circular stone with a hole through the centre large enough to crawl through. Thought to date from the Bronze Age, around three to four thousand years ago, it is possible that the stones once formed part of a circle since others have been found nearby, but the visual symbolism intended here is unequivocal. These stones have long been associated with fertility and well-being. Engagements between young couples were sealed here at New Year by holding hands through the stone and, at the right times of the lunar month, it was believed that fertility could be assured by clambering through the hole nine times. Until relatively recently, rituals were performed to restore the health of sick infants or to ensure an easy childbirth.

And in the far north, barely a mile to the south-east of the Ring of Brodgar on Orkney, are the magnificent Stones of Stenness. Silhouetted against the midsummer sunset these stones tower, straight-sided, like inverted guillotine blades. The tallest of these beautifully grained sandstone slabs is nearly six metres high but, at a width of just thirty centimetres, their height is exaggerated by their incredible thinness. To erect this circle without snapping them was a significant engineering feat. Only four stones now survive and one of those has been snapped off just above ground level, but originally there was space for twelve. Mysteriously, a socket was never found for the twelfth stone and it is believed that a gap was left at the south-east – the direction of the midwinter sunrise. By 1760 all but four uprights had been lost and its crescent-shaped arrangement led the Stones of Stenness to be known as the Temple of the Moon.

The interior of the circle once held an upright timber post at the centre, reminiscent, perhaps of the phallic pillars at the Sanctuary or the stone Obelisk at Avebury. This was replaced at some stage by a four-sided stone cove in what seems like a shift in emphasis from male to female symbolism.

The Stenness Circle was a traditional place for young islanders to make their betrothals. From here, they would make their way one hundred and fifty metres to the north of the circle where a single holed stone, known as the Odin Stone, stood. Tradition then required them to 'proceed to consummation without further ceremony'. Declarations of intent made by clasping hands through the hole were considered binding. One woman from the nearby village of Stromness pledged her love at the Odin Stone with her pirate sweetheart. When he was

The Stones of Stenness on mainland Orkney was an auspicious place to consummate a marriage.

hanged for piracy in Greenwich in 1725 she travelled seven hundred miles to London to hold his dead hand and thereby be released from the vow. Despite its traditional significance to young couples on Orkney, for reasons unknown, in 1814 the landowner destroyed the Odin Stone.

The chamber entrance of the West Kennet barrow lies at the eastern end of the burial mound facing the warming rays of the morning sun and guarded by a daunting rank of vertical stone orthostats.

CHAPTER THREE

From the Womb to the Tomb

AN EARLY SYMBOL WAS THE CAVE WHICH EXTENDS INTO THE MOTHERLY EARTH FROM WHICH ALL LIFE ARISES. THE CAVE REPRESENTS THE FIRST SPATIAL ELEMENT. ARTIFICIAL CAVES WERE CREATED AS DOLMENS.

STUART PIGGOTT

Sex and death are two subjects not often associated in the minds of modern people but this was not always the case. In south-east Asia, Rangda, the mythological goddess of sex, was also influential in matters of the departed; and in the folklore of ancient Wales, female deities known as Cerridwen and Blodeuwedd governed both death and the antithetical process of regeneration. But if we want stronger proof that the concepts of sex and death were once entwined in past cultures we must delve inside the earthy confines of a prehistoric burial chamber.

The West Kennet barrow is a magnificent burial mound less than a mile to the south of the great stone circle of Avebury in the English Wiltshire Downs. At over 100 metres in length, this is one of the largest, best preserved and most famous communal tombs of its kind in the British Isles. It was built over five and a half thousand years ago in a superbly elevated position along the crest of a high chalk ridge. Oriented east to west in line with the sun's path across the sky, this gigantic mound must have presented an imposing profile on the skyline. When the barrow was eventually excavated, a wealth of information was retrieved, not only about its structure, but also the people who lay buried within it; some astonishing facts were also brought to light about the rituals and beliefs of these prehistoric tomb builders.

Walking up on to this ridge the barrow lies like a green-hulled ship marooned in a sea of waving corn. The chamber entrance lies at the eastern end of the barrow, facing the warming rays of the early morning sun and guarded by a daunting rank of vertical stone slabs, or orthostats. Despite the breeze rustling the long grass on the mound, the inside of the tomb is silent and still. A stone-lined passage extends into the body of the earthen mound, with two chambers opening to either side. It culminates in a fifth rounded chamber and the entire subterranean space is covered by enormously heavy capstones. The dark walls of the passage are clammy and cold and the air, even on a hot day, feels distinctly chilled.

Bones belonging to a total of forty-six individuals were eventually recovered during excavation. As was common in Neolithic times, the bodies had been exposed until all flesh had disappeared before the remains were conveyed into the tomb. Each of the five chambers held bones that had been carefully sorted and arranged in heaps according to sex and age. Strangely, though, many of the bones were missing. It is possible that some were lost as the bodies were moved after de-fleshing but the skulls and long bones in particular were conspicuously absent. Here, it would appear, was the source of the

bones used in the grisly fertility rituals at the Avebury stone circle.

The universal cycle of rebirth was being enacted as the sunrise shone on the east-facing stones of the West Kennet chamber. In a practice mirrored by cultures as diverse as those of North American Indians and European Christians, the dead were placed with reference to the dawn, whose first rays brought regenerating warmth and light. The only articulated body to be found was that of an elderly man. This unfortunate individual had suffered in life with deformed toes and an abscess on his shoulder. One of his arms was fractured at the time of his death but it was undoubtedly an arrow in the neck that had proved fatal. He, too, was laid in the cold stone chamber at the eastern end of the mound but carefully placed in the foetal position, perhaps to facilitate his eventual rebirth.

But it was not only the remains of humans that were buried on top of the hill. In many societies, oxen are regarded as sacred animals. Perhaps because they are ubiquitously yoked to ploughs that till the fertile soil they have also been long associated with the fecundity of the earth itself. This dubious honour has led to their sacrifice in many cultures to secure the favour of deities who controlled the fruitfulness of the people, their animals and the soil. Several ox phalanges, or foot bones, were recovered from the

To prehistoric people, the compact rounded mound of Cuween chambered tomb was the pregnant belly and uterus of a fertile earth goddess.

West Kennet long barrow. Carved chalk phalluses have been found in other burial mounds such as Winterborne Stoke and Thickthorn on Salisbury Plain and it is possible that the ox phalanges were selected for their distinctly phallic shape.

Outside the entrance to the tomb lay a low, crescent-shaped forecourt. Its function, it seems, was that of a stage where rituals may have been performed before a crowd gathered in front of the barrow. The shape of the horned forecourt reflects the horns of the ox – a powerful symbol associated with fertility throughout Indo-European cultures.

Beyond the forecourt stretched the earthen length of the barrow. Deep ditches cut down either side provided a mass of chalk rubble for the construction of a mound that, when new, would have shone dazzlingly white. Excavation in the 1950s exposed a narrow central core of local sandstone boulders extending down the length of the mound. Short, paired lines of stones were also discovered projecting from this at right angles, like ribs from a sandstone spine. The West Kennet barrow was clearly more than a mound of earth. The burial chambers intrude into just one eighth of the total overall length of a great tapering mound with no evident structural role. Its design is more architecturally sophisticated than was necessary to cover the remains of the dead, so why did the builders of West Kennet go to so much extra effort in constructing this tomb?

In Shetland and in Northern Ireland, two Neolithic plaques have been found that archaeologists believe may provide an answer to the intricately constructed mound. Carved from bone and stone the plaques are trapezoidal in shape with a narrow line down each long edge. The widest ends are slightly curved, one with an indentation in the centre. Both plaques have been beautifully engraved but, amazingly, the Irish artefact is scored with a central line up the long axis from which delicate lines run at right angles.

The similarities between these plaques and the structure of the West Kennet barrow are striking. The trapezoidal plan of the barrow, the flanking ditches and internal stone structure are all echoed in the finely engraved lines. Even the indentation coincides convincingly with the passage entrance at West Kennet, but what do the designs of the barrow and plaques mean? The surface of the Shetland plaque is incised with a series of hatched geometric patterns. This abstract art is reminiscent of designs that occur widely throughout the prehistoric graves of Britain and Ireland and that have been interpreted as representing the female pubic triangle. Archaeologists now believe that the trapezoidal plaques depict a highly stylised figure of a fertile mother goddess.

What was built on the hill near Avebury, it would seem, was not just a burial mound but a symbolic body of the mother goddess. Her earthen length lay pure white and supine along the crest of the ridge, the horns of the forecourt protruding like legs between which the passage led into a dark, incubating womb. Ancestors were returned to the safety of her enfolding body. The high degree of ritual and care that surrounded the deposition of the dead suggests that prehistoric people held a belief in some form of afterlife. Inside the goddess, the bones of the dead lay in their chamber, covered by her rounded, pregnant belly awaiting the penetrating, life-bringing rays of the sun – and rebirth.

The interior of Cuween chambered tomb held a collection of skulls and long bones that may have been used in sexual rites.

After spending some time within the sombre, airless confines of the chamber, to emerge from the passageway into the light and warmth outside is like experiencing birth itself. It is incredible to think that people depositing the bones of their community members five thousand years ago surely had exactly the same feeling as they stepped out once more into the sun. After the bones of many generations had been brought to West Kennet, at the end of nearly one and a half thousand years of use, the tomb was ritually sealed. The chambers were filled with rich, fertile earth appropriate for the body of the mother goddess, and the entrance blocked with the huge upright stone slabs still in place today.

Long earthen mounds like West Kennet were constructed across the uplands of southern England as places not only for the dead but where rituals vital to continued existence could be performed by the living. And there are numerous variations in design of the goddess womb, such as Cuween, one of Orkney's lesser known, but most enchanting sites.

The Orkney mainland, lying at the point where the waters of the North Sea merge with the swirling Atlantic Ocean, is an exposed but fertile island whose patchwork of small fields has been farmed since the Neolithic Age. In a supremely elevated position, high on the eastern slopes of the Hill of Heddle with incredible views over the blue, wind-whipped waters of the Bay of Firth, is the superbly built chambered tomb of Cuween. On days when clouds are being driven across the sky, the wind up here can be almost too strong to stand against. To then duck into the passageway under the mound is to enter a world of immediate stillness that is dizzying after being buffeted outside.

Cuween is a small tomb but its architecture more than makes up for in style what it lacks in size. The intimate scale of the small main chamber, which can be spanned with outstretched arms, feels appropriate for the delicately thin layers of Orcadian flagstone that form the walls and beautifully corbelled roof. Even after a dry spell the stones inside are damp to the touch, and without artificial illumination the blackness is oppressive. In each of the four walls is an opening into a tiny, stone-lined side chamber. Twenty-four dog skulls were discovered in the tomb – the carefully placed remains of a community's totemic animal. The remains of five humans were also found here, represented, in an exact reversal of West Kennet, by only their skulls and thighbones. That these particular bones were selected for deposition suggests that similar, sexually symbolic ceremonies took place here on Orkney.

Bearing in mind what Neolithic societies seem to have been communicating in their construction of

Dunchraigaig cairn: 'a fulsome uproarious feminine cleft, a mother slit in the side of the big cairn belly. The great capstone . . . protrudes from the inside like megalithic labia' — Julian Cope.

these tombs, the body of mother earth at Cuween is particularly well formed. This compact, rounded mound is a tight, pregnant belly of earth and stones and the symbolism intended in the narrow passageway would not have required explanation in a culture where such metaphor was deeply rooted in tradition. In their ancient cosmology these burial places were not just designed to look like the womb of a great earth goddess – they *were* the womb of a great earth goddess.

Twelve thousand years ago, the west coast of Scotland was still in the grip of an ice age. The valley that now holds the tranquil waters of Loch Awe then contained a vast, mountain-scouring glacier. When the

A hillside platform overlooked the Kintraw phallus that brought fertility and rebirth to the adjacent burial cairn.

ice eventually melted, floodwaters roared through the Kilmartin Glen to the south depositing whole terraces of waterborne sand and gravel on their way to the sea. In time these fertile terraced slopes, descending to the floor of one of Britain's prettiest valleys, provided an agricultural Utopia where early farmers chose to settle and grow their crops. Eventually it is where they were buried.

Here, at the foot of the slopes of Barr na Saille, a stream slowly meanders through a fabulously rich prehistoric landscape. The ground between its watery loops is packed with ancient sites: a ceremonial enclosure, cup-marked standing stones, an outstanding example of prehistoric rock art – and the chambered cairn of Dunchraigaig.

Dunchraigaig itself is a remarkable monument. Its mound of great boulders and water-washed pebbles was excavated in 1864 by an enthusiastic antiquarian named Canon William Greenwell. Visitors today could be forgiven for not at first recognising the covert sexuality embodied by these stones. The ceremonial importance of the tomb was made clear, however, by Greenwell's discovery of artefacts including a flint knife and a fine greenstone axe – prized objects that would have been of ritual rather than purely practical value to their owners.

Although now disturbed and overgrown with turf, it is the form of the monument itself that is so intriguing. The entrance to the mound is exquisite. A narrow, dark slit is overlain by a wide stone lintel in an arrangement described by one prehistorian as 'a fulsome uproarious feminine cleft, a mother slit in the side of the big cairn belly. The great capstone that holds all the structure in place protrudes from the inside like megalithic labia and the chamber of a Neolithic cairn has never before been quite so . . . sexual'. If a twenty-first century eye can appreciate innuendo in a pile of stones then how much more palpable must the symbolism have been to Neolithic

settlers whose culture was steeped in the sexually charged atmosphere of these ritual sites?

On the island of Anglesey, in the shadow of the great mountain of Snowdon, is a landscape that seems deeply imbued with sacred meaning. Here, the swollen outline of Bryn-Celli-Ddu, a vast burial mound, rises from the ground, draped in a soft mantle of downy grass. Some distance from the mound, beyond a natural rocky outcrop where a seat – perhaps used in rituals – has been worn by the elements, stands a craggy pillar of stone known as Llanddaniel Fab Menhir. The stone, seat and mound are all perfectly aligned, suggesting that they were collectively significant in a ritual landscape, but if this phallic pillar had intentions of courting the womb of Bryn-Celli-Ddu then it has literally been left out in the cold. Another stone column – a smooth, round-headed stone – was erected in the very depths of the uterine tomb. It is impossible not to imagine that this monolithic phallus was intended to fertilise the depths of the female goddess's womb, lending its virile forces to the incubating belly of the earth. And, as if leaving nothing to chance, its superstitious builders also interred an entire ox carcass under the floor facing the entrance to the tomb.

On a tight bend in the winding coast road, overlooking the head of Loch Craignish in Scotland's mid-Argyll region, lies a tumbled pile of rocks. Now

The Kintraw standing stone overlooks both Craignish and the breast-shaped Paps of Jura on Scotland's west coast.

used by sheep as a windbreak, this is what remains of a once great burial cairn – though it was not always so dilapidated. Human bones that had been cremated and carefully placed buried in a cist were uncovered here along with vast quantities of quartz in the area around the cairn, which must have shimmered like gems in the sunlight when first built. The mound is a touching reminder that prehistoric people treated their dead with honour and ceremony, but these stones were not the only ones to be placed on this small plateau above the loch.

The magnificent and controversial Kintraw stone, a towering column of red stone, also stands on this terrace between the sea and the hills. On a clear day, the Paps of Jura – outrageously breast-shaped hills twenty-seven miles distant across the Sound of Jura – would have formed the backdrop for a spectacular performance. In a composition which eloquently brought together the elements of mountains, sun, water and stone, prehistoric architects erected the Kintraw stone in perfect alignment with the midwinter sunset. The setting sun, on the shortest day of the year, would have sunk behind the Paps of Jura, perhaps witnessed from a platform in the hillside behind the stone. Before darkness, though, the sun reappears, blazing for a moment in the cleavage between the hills, before finally setting again. Within view of the sacred mountainous Paps, the Kintraw

The distinctive sweeping lines of Maes
Howe rise like a gigantic wide-brimmed
hat but its core is evidence of Neolithic
sophistication.

stone was erected as a symbol of impregnating power,
a fertilising shaft that, perhaps in shadow form, added
its virility to the mounded burial womb.

The sun was certainly an important element in the
design of prehistoric burial places as centres of
fertility and of rebirth. Many tombs throughout the
British Isles were built to honour the rising and setting
of the sun on auspicious dates throughout the year,
and there is perhaps no finer example than Maes
Howe on the Scottish island of Orkney.

Named M'eshoo by the Vikings and mentioned in
the epic account of the Orkneyinga Saga, the tomb
dates back to a time four thousand years before these
Norse raiders broke into the chamber and left their

59

graffiti scrawled on its walls. Maes Howe, renowned as the finest megalithic tomb in north-western Europe, is also the largest cairn of its type in Scotland. It was built on an artificially levelled platform by the southern shores of the Loch of Harray by a society who can be identified through their use of a distinctively decorated style of pottery known as Grooved Ware. These people lived in settlements like Skara Brae and performed their ceremonies at the nearby Stones of Stenness, less than a mile away around the water-lapped edge of the loch.

The distinctive mound of Maes Howe rises from the peaceful, cow-grazed fields like a gigantic wide-brimmed hat, but its simple sweeping lines hide a core that is evidence of the astonishing sophistication of its Neolithic builders. The square-sectioned passageway is lined with sharp-edged blocks shaped so neatly before being fitted together that it is impossible to slip even a knife blade between them. Nine metres in length, the passage can be just about entered bent double; one Viking raider left a scrawled pun about a haughty woman stooping to enter here.

It emerges into a magnificent, high-ceilinged vault with walls and a corbelled roof of Orcadian flagstones, put together entirely without the use of mortar. From each of the four walls a waist-high portal opens into a small side chamber and on the floor below each opening lie the finely tapered stones that were used to seal these chambers. Part of the way along the entrance passage is a recess in the wall. It houses a block of stone estimated to weigh at least one tonne but which is said to be so carefully placed as to be moved with the pressure from just one finger. Most curious of all, the doorway was designed to be closed from *inside* the tomb, conjuring images of rites too sacred to be observed.

In summer, the Northern Isles enjoy almost twenty-four hour daylight but in winter the situation is reversed. Days pass when the sun barely skims the horizon and the nights would seem endlessly long. This point in the depth of winter when the sun begins its slow return to the skies would have held great significance for these prehistoric people of the north. It represented hope of a renewed fertility and a return to the life-giving warmth of spring. The passageway at Maes Howe was carefully aligned to the south-west so that once a year, at sunset on the midwinter solstice, the last rays of the setting sun entered through a slit in the door stone. The back wall of the chamber would be lit by an orange beam in a silent theatre of light and symbolic penetration of the dark womb.

It is not known how many people's bones were eventually housed in the chamber at Maes Howe; an excavation in 1861 recovered only one piece of human skull. The contents may have been cleared out by Vikings who, in the twelfth century AD, broke in through the roof of the tomb. These Norsemen covered the walls in scribblings deemed to be the best collection of runes anywhere in the world. Some of their messages betray suspicions that the mound once held a rich burial hoard; others, such as 'Thorni bedded Helgi', are simply timeless.

The symbolic male power of the winter solstice sun was widely acknowledged throughout the British Isles. At Sliabh na Callighe, or Loughcrew, in County Meath in Ireland a vast complex of Neolithic passage tombs, one of the largest in Ireland, was discovered in the 1860s. Along a curving spine of high ground – the watershed between the Boyne and Shannon Rivers rise three hilltops. In full view and, therefore, in constant mind, this prominent horizon is where local Neolithic people returned their dead to the womb of mother earth in a necropolis of over thirty tombs.

The name Carnbane, or White Mound, also given to the site is a reference to the brilliant quartz that covered the surfaces of the burial mounds. One of these, the unassumingly named Cairn T was built on the highest point in County Meath and is one of the most spectacular monuments on this exposed ridge. The rugged stony exterior gives no clues to the meticulous architecture of the chamber deep inside the mound. A short passageway opens into a magnificent cruciform chamber with sills set into the

The setting sun at midwinter penetrates the Maes Howe passage bringing light and the hope of regeneration to the darkest months of the year.

61

The tombs at Loughcrew command expansive views across the fertile plains of Ireland's Boyne and Shannon rivers.

floor that must be stepped over upon entering as though making the point that a special space is being entered.

The monuments were positioned on the hilltop for maximum dramatic effect. Cairn T was constructed with the passage entrance opening onto a small natural platform that could be used for rituals associated with the deposition of the dead, but its orientation also had other theatrical advantages. Twice a year, at dawn on the vernal equinox in late March, and again at the autumn equinox in September, the first rays of the morning sun shine directly down the passage. The beam of light enters the chamber in a very graphic penetration of the tomb and illuminates an intricately carved slab known as the Equinox Stone.

Loughcrew boasts some of the most beautiful and intricately carved passage grave art in Ireland. The walls of the tomb are incised with radial patterns like a large, spoked sun. There are circles and spirals believed to be associated with the Neolithic belief in the continuance of life through cycles of fertility and rebirth. And there are curious linear designs, like numerical tallies, comprising one central line with short marks made along its length at right angles. It is tempting to wonder at a connection between these linear carvings and the goddess plan seen in the architecture of long earthen barrows like West Kennet.

If Neolithic tombs were the embodiment of a mother goddess then she is portrayed not only as life-giving but also as devourer of the dead. Later Celtic societies believed in a trinity of goddesses – the incarnate forms of Maiden, Mother and Hag. Here at Loughcrew, the remarkable naming of one feature may suggest that the origins of this trinity lie further back in history than any records can show. One of the kerbstones of Cairn T is an enormous block of stone. There is no way of knowing whether this rock, with its seat-like ledge and arm rests, was chosen deliberately for its shape but at some point in the past it was named the Hag's Chair. Legend also maintains that the entire

Loughcrew's Equinox Stone: passage grave art deep within the tomb may be connected to fertility and regeneration and is illuminated twice a year by the equinoctial dawn.

burial complex, known locally as Hag's Hill, was formed when three piles of stone were dropped from a crone's apron as she flew over.

Not far to the east of Loughcrew is an area known as the Brú na Bóinne, or 'dwelling place of the Boyne'. Here, the River Boyne meanders in dramatic loops through an ancient landscape where prehistoric henges jostle for space with standing stones and medieval cemeteries, testifying to the length of

occupation in this area. But it is for its magnificent Neolithic passage graves that the Brú na Bóinne is most renowned.

Sí an Bhrú, or Newgrange – one of the most spectacular prehistoric monuments in Western Europe – dominates the landscape. More than five thousand years old, this enormous burial mound of stone and earth covers an entire acre of ground and its perimeter is surrounded by no less than ninety-seven kerbstones. One of these, a huge recumbent stone at the entrance to the passage, is entirely covered with elegantly carved spirals, diamonds and swirls. A stone-lined passage extends from here deep into the body of the mound culminating, at the centre, in a cross-shaped chamber. Some of the most elaborate grave art in the world can be found on these tomb walls. Many of the designs at Newgrange appear in triplicate and the most beautiful of these is found at the end of the chamber where, meticulously carved into a stone, are three entwined spirals. Tracing with a finger from the centre of one leads directly into the adjacent spiral. This design has been interpreted as depicting the cyclical nature of life, death, and perhaps even rebirth.

To the later Celts, three was a profoundly sacred number. It reflected the trinity of goddesses they worshipped and the obsessive repetition of triplicate designs at sacred places like Newgrange may testify to an even earlier belief in the significance of the divine threesome. Here, then was an abstract depiction of a mother goddess associated not only with death, but with the vital process of regeneration and who, most importantly, could be entreated to ensure the fertility of those still living.

At dawn on the morning of the midwinter solstice, a beam of light enters the Newgrange passage through a narrow slit above the door known as the roof-box. As its rays penetrate deeper into the vaginal tomb, suddenly the entire underground chamber is filled with a fireball of orange light that illuminates the triple spiral carving with a supernatural glow. The effect lasts only moments but this symbolic penetration of the body of the goddess of death by a life-bringing shaft of light from the male sun god surely brought a long, awe-filled silence to those gathered here on a chilly December morning five thousand years ago.

Returning the dead to the belly of the earth was evidently undertaken by early farmers in the Brú na Bóinne with great attention to ceremony. Not surprisingly, perhaps, in the face of beliefs that ancestors were a tangible link to the forces of nature that could nurture or destroy the living, there is evidence that an even deeper but much more subtle symbolism was sometimes embedded within these wombs of the goddess.

The Hag's Chair at Loughcrew may be a folklore reference to the earth goddess in her final incarnation as ancient crone.

Just across the fields to the north-west of Newgrange lies another superb burial mound known as Knowth. Curiously, the construction of the outer tomb wall involved a sophisticated use of geological material that went beyond local resources. Sherds of brilliant white quartz were included in the wall fabric, as were black stones known as granodiorite. Silt-stone cobbles streaked with blue and white were also found, creating an effect that was as visually impressive as it was puzzling. Why would such care be taken to include these coloured stones – and what did they signify?

The decorated kerbstone at the entrance to Newgrange lies in front of the roof-box through which a narrow beam of light graphically penetrates the tomb.

Research into similar geological occurrences in tombs on the Isle of Arran in Scotland has led to the tentative suggestion that it is actually possible to infer meaning from the colours of the stones. Red sandstone from the coastal plain has been used in contexts involving blood, flesh and fertility; white rocks appear to symbolise the bleached appearance of bones left exposed to the elements; and black pitchstone has been associated with places of darkness and death. At Knowth, it seems, was a language coded in colour and designed to symbolise the various aspects of the cycle of sex and death. Here, the desire to impregnate and bring rebirth was brought down to a more recognisably human scale. A life-sized stone phallus was recovered from a burial chamber, carved with intricate grooves and clearly intended to be interred deep underground as a potent sexual symbol.

In the far north-east of the Scottish mainland, a dead straight road cuts, unfenced, through a land of high heather moors and grazing sheep past the Grey Cairns of Camster. Once standing as three separate stone cairns, two adjacent mounds were merged at some stage into one enormous long cairn. Now crows hover, ragged and motionless in the wind, over the undulating conjoined mass of stones whose height tails off to the south like the lithe outline of a reclining figure.

These superb cairns – made more magnificent by their bleak location – are reached by wooden boardwalks across a moor sodden even in the height of summer and flecked with a host of tufted heads of cotton-grass. The lowest stone courses of the long cairn and its flanking horned forecourts are of neatly laid flagstones. As though its builders tired of this precision, the rest of the mound was completed as a jumbled pile of irregularly shaped rocks. For just a few minutes each day, at sunrise and again at sunset, the distinctive colour of the stones, which earned this site its name, turns from grey to warm, glowing orange.

Both chambers of the conjoined cairns can be entered by crawling along their short passageways. Originally topped by fine corbelled roofs, these vaults

are like miniature, domed cathedrals; indeed, at the head of one chamber is a vast, smooth stone like a two-dimensional church altar. Despite their cramped approaches and diminutive interiors these chambers have a strange acoustic appeal.

Perhaps in response to this, an experiment was carried out to investigate the effects of sound inside the single round cairn at Camster. Amazingly, it was demonstrated that drumming within the echoing confines of the tomb could produce levels of sound too low to be detected by the human ear but which could be detected physically as vibrations. It is tempting to think that resonating sound was used to great effect in the rituals of death and rebirth played out amongst the stones.

When ancient people buried their dead in these earthen womblike spaces they were inextricably bonding their ancestors to the fecundity of the soil. The spirits of the dead inhabited the interface between the tangible world of the living and that of the capricious forces of Nature. Tombs were built as sensory theatres in which symbolically-coloured stones and pungent earthy smells merged with the intoxicating rhythms of resonating sound to such sensory effect that any chanting or ritual activities would have taken place in an atmosphere already charged with awe and expectation. In the animistic minds of early farmers, adherence to these

The Grey Cairns of Camster have acoustic properties that would have added a physical element to ceremonies held inside.

ceremonial activities involving the bones of their ancestors was fundamental to the fertility of the land. Later, feast days associated with harvests and fertility, such as Michaelmas, would became merged with festivals to honour the dead.

Until the later medieval period, the acts of preparing and planting the soil were traditionally steeped in sexual symbolism. The land was the female body of a goddess. Ploughing a furrow was the ultimate penetrative act, usually carried out by males. The introduction of seeds also had obvious connotations. The intimate connection between the fecundity of women and the fertility of the soil cannot be overstated; in the minds of early farmers, the two were the same. In many cultures it was customary for men to masturbate over the soil prior to the first season's planting in order to ensure the success of the crop.

But men and women did not always play separate roles in these pre-planting fertility rites. One account records that 'For four days before they committed the seed to the earth the Pipiles of Central America kept apart from their wives in order that on the night before planting they might indulge their passion to the fullest extent; certain persons are even said to have been appointed to perform the sexual act at the very moment when the first seeds were deposited in the ground.' As art imitates life, examples of European rock art demonstrate the graphic and literal connection between ploughing, planting and sexuality. And ploughing was not the only time that cutting into the ground seems to have been infused with sexual meaning.

Roughly halfway along the West Kennet Avenue at Avebury is an area identified as being of great archaeological interest. A series of small pits were dug here and into them some very curious objects were placed: the skull of an ox, with its implied associations with fertility rites, and charcoal from hazel and hawthorn shrubs that flower in spring and bear fruit in the autumn. Indeed, all the contents of the pit have been interpreted as being connected in some way to the cycles of reproduction. If this route was taken by young women on their way to a springtime union inside the main stone circle at Avebury then it is not surprising that fruitfulness was high on the agenda.

At Windmill Hill, just north of Avebury, further evidence has been found of a connection between sex and holes in the ground. This Neolithic enclosure, one of the earliest yet to be recognised in the country, was used as a regional centre for both trade and festivals. Such a large site would have drawn people from a wide area to take part in or observe the mysterious ceremonies around which the existence of these early farmers revolved and which, it seems, were decidedly adult in content.

The Clava Cairns of Balnuaran have distinctly womb-shaped interiors.

Sixty chalk balls small enough to sit in the palm of a hand have been recovered from the ditch surrounding the site. These could be interpreted as having a variety of practical or symbolic uses – but they were found in pairs. Four items identified as carved phalluses have also been found which, 'in that uncircumcised age could hardly be more explicit, the exposed glans showing that the penis was supposed to be in a state of erection'. These model penises were intricately carved with the heads being defined by a delicate groove. Blocks of chalk into which cup-like depressions had been carved were also discovered and these, in such a provocative context, have tentatively been interpreted as abstract depictions of female genitalia. The distribution of these finds, buried within the sites, suggests that they were ritually placed – objects of desire closely bonding the fertility of the land with human sexuality.

Today people come to the Norfolk Brecklands to ramble through acres of forest and perhaps to catch a glimpse of some of the heath's shyer occupants – the lizards, woodlarks and roe deer. To the region's inhabitants five thousand years ago, however, the most important natural resource lay deep underground.

From the north coast of Norfolk to the English Channel stretches one of the broadest geological bands of chalk in Britain – but it was seams of flint deep within this chalk that attracted the first miners to the Brecklands. Flint is an extremely hard rock chemically similar to glass, which can be chipped, or knapped, to form a razor-sharp cutting edge. A valuable resource for early settlers, it was essential in making tools for clearing the virgin forests of hazel, lime and oak, for hunting and for defence. But the veins of precious jet-black flint were mined in a process that seems to have been far from straightforward extraction.

Neolithic flint mines at a site known as Grimes Graves lie at the heart of this Norfolk chalkland. On a summer's day skylarks can be heard high overhead and the ground is swathed with the yellow flowers of vetch and rock rose, every step pungently scenting the air with wild thyme. But the ground itself is scarred and pitted with huge craters like a battlefield or the surface of the moon. Anglo-Saxons believed that such a place could only be the work of the god Grim, and named it after him. Darker forces were also implicated, as the site was variously known as the Devil's Holes but for centuries the true origins of this bizarre landscape were a complete mystery. Then in 1868 Canon William Greenwell carried out the first scientific excavation of one of the deepest shafts with some very surprising results.

Over a period of perhaps five hundred years many hundreds of shafts were dug in one of the largest known flint extraction sites in Britain. Descending deep into the earth on wooden ladders, these Stone Age miners were armed with only deer-antler picks and wooden shovels. The deepest pits were up to fourteen metres deep, but, cut into brilliant white chalk and open to the sky, enough reflected sunlight would have reached the bottom of the shaft for the miners to work by. A warren of tunnels radiated from the shaft base often no more half a metre high, and crawling along these to quarry and drag out the heavy nodules of flint would have been unenviable work. But finds uncovered by Greenwell, and since then during more recent excavations, suggest that the mining process here was deeply imbued with sexual ritual.

At the bottom of what is now known as Greenwell's Pit the skull of a phalarope was found. This wading bird, now a migrant visitor to the shores of East Anglia, must have been deliberately brought inland to Grimes Graves where it was carefully laid on the chalk floor with along with a pair of antler picks and a carved chalk phallus. Seventy years later, Leslie Armstrong was investigating the bottom of another shaft when he made a similar discovery. Upon a low chalk mound, seven antler picks had been arranged with carved chalk phalluses and pairs of chalk balls. Armstrong was also famously attributed with recovering a controversial 'goddess' figurine. This voluptuous female statuette with broad hips and pendulous breasts is reminiscent of earlier,

The pitted landscape at Grimes Graves in Norfolk is what remains of a prehistoric industrial flint-extraction process that was deeply imbued with sexual ritual.

Chalk phalluses and pairs of chalk balls were found at the entrances to galleries and tunnels deep underground at Grimes Graves.

so-called 'Venus' figurines from Eastern Europe. But the statuette, as an archaeological source, must be treated with caution, since Armstrong's lover at the time he excavated the pit was a sculptress and the figurine was found just after she had left the site. He is reputed to have ended their relationship the following day.

So what does all this mean? These carefully placed ritual deposits have forced archaeologists to rethink their interpretation of the whole flint-mining industry and parallels have subsequently been drawn with mining by North American Indians for the red stone used to make their ceremonial pipes. Pipestone was deeply sacred and believed to symbolise the Native

American people. In 1836 the words of one Indian were committed to record: 'You see [holding a red pipe to the side of his naked arm] that this pipe is a part of our flesh. The red men are a part of the red stone.' The stem of the pipe was regarded as male, the bowl female, and the tobacco they burned and imbibed represented the very earth itself. In the mythology of the Arapaho, the spirit Nih'ancan created the earth from the first pipe and used it to create men and women. Before quarrying the sacred stone, miners had to be ritually purified in a sweat lodge and their tools were smudged with burning sage to cleanse them. Offerings were also made near the quarry to mediate with spirits before any stone was removed from the body of the mother earth. Is it possible that flint mining in Norfolk was similarly veiled in ritual and meaning?

Good quality flint was readily available at Grimes Graves just beneath the surface of the ground and yet the miners undertook the perilous task of extracting this valuable resource from deep underground. Given that many ritual deposits were found at entrances to tunnels it seems that the activity of penetrating the earth was symbolic in itself. Entering the cool, claustrophobic semi-darkness of the mines would have been an experience comparable above ground only to the act of entering a burial chamber, suggesting that here, too, the earth was equated with the body of the

goddess. To enter a tunnel would seem to prehistoric miners like penetrating the womb of mother earth.

The bird skull has been interpreted as a reference to the sky. Placed deep within the ground it may have symbolised a sexual union between the male sky gods and the female earth to encourage the production of the precious, black resource. Perhaps, as in North America, permission was sought before removing the flint they relied upon and the ritual deposits represented gifts offered in exchange for the raw material taken. If a shaft was particularly productive then offerings may have been made in thanks. Or tokens could have been left in tunnels that failed to yield the expected quantity of much-needed flint to encourage more fruitful results in the next shaft. The entire process was loaded with metaphors of fertility and renewal.

Burial chambers and mining shafts were clearly endowed with powerful meaning by their creators, but were built in imitation of features within the natural landscape. Caves and grottoes seem to have been revered from the earliest times as profoundly sacred spaces. Throughout Europe, where subterranean passages have been found leading deep underground, there is evidence that prehistoric people entered the body of the earth – and attached ritual importance to the experience. With only dim illumination from smoky flames, people penetrated entire European cave systems where, in the half-light, they daubed elaborate paintings on a canvas of stone. Along with their art, they left behind footprints and, occasionally, items that have led archaeologists to believe that ceremonies took place deep underground. Adolescent boys may have entered these dark passages to undergo unknown rites of initiation within the dark, uterine spaces of the earth. Afterwards they would have emerged back into the light, reborn as young men of the tribe.

In Scotland the tiny Hebridean island of Eigg, barely five miles as the crow flies from its northern to its southern tip, bravely pokes above the waters of the Cuillin Sound just south of Skye. Its remote northeast coast is a rugged, scree-lined shore where the waves incessantly tear at the foot of cliffs formed of towering basalt columns. Here, amid the boulders on a platform of made-up ground, lies a small, circular enclosure. Its interior, just six or so paces in diameter, opens into a natural cave with further, smaller side chambers. Animal bones, shells and fragments of hammer-stones littered the floor but this was no ordinary prehistoric dwelling place.

Nestled between two great chunks of rock that protrude from the shore like bent knees, the round enclosure may have been built to emphasise the opening into what has been interpreted as a ritual cavern. In a landscape of endless rock and stone, the

Stone steps at the prehistoric site of Mine Howe descend below ground to a series of ceremonial chambers.

Just metres from a modern road can be found the entrance to an Iron Age souterrain at Culsh in Aberdeenshire.

cliff-line at this particular point displays a marked change in geology. We already know that prehistoric people had a subtle awareness of mineralogical detail, and exploited variations in stone type in the building of their circles such as those on Machrie Moor. At this place 'where the horizontal bands of rock are broken by a great thrust of vertical basalt columns' were the

ancient inhabitants of the island of Eigg invoking a symbolic union between the phallic basalt columns and vaginal cavern?

If caves were indeed regarded as highly ritual places then an answer may have been found to some of the most mysterious prehistoric sites in Britain. In the spring of 1946 an opening was found in a massive

At Carn Euny in Cornwall, an underground passage links to a chamber strikingly similar to a native North American sweat lodge.

natural mound in the east of mainland Orkney. A perilously steep flight of stone steps led down into the earth from the mound but the significance of the remains was not recognised and the steps were covered over. More than fifty years later, what is now thought to be a symbolic passage into the prehistoric netherworld was re-excavated.

Twenty-seven narrow steps descend into the ground at Mine Howe. From a landing half way down, two horizontal galleries are carved out of solid bedrock and the stairs then spiral back, dropping down to a lower chamber almost seven metres below the entrance. The darkness in this deepest chamber of the man-made cave is almost total. Above, the roof of

The labyrinthine maze of tunnels and chambers at Halliggye fogou echoes an early symbol associated with the cycles of birth and regeneration.

overlapping Orcadian flagstone is reminiscent of a corbelled tomb and excavation records reveal that 'hundreds of bones and other relics were strewn about the floor of this chamber' including cockleshells and 'curious polished stones'. The exact age of the underground chambers at Mine Howe has not yet been discerned, and light will possibly never be shed on the ceremonies performed with bones and shells deep within the womb of the goddess.

Another, similarly enigmatic type of monuments is found in Cornwall and more widely throughout Scotland. Known in the north as 'souterrains' from the French meaning 'underground', these musty, stone-lined passages, thought to be over two thousand years old, lead down into the earth in the most surprising places. In woodlands and back gardens, a hole – often just large enough to crawl through, is the only trace on the surface of these subterranean tunnelings. Some have side chambers or intricate, winding passages but all culminate, mysteriously, in a dead end.

Near Tarland in Aberdeenshire an aperture beside the road, easily large enough to crawl through, is the entrance to the Culsh souterrain. A gently curving tunnel roughly sixteen metres in length is roofed with gigantic stones. The walls, of smooth slabs, are covered in a fine moss that, where the light shines on it, appears like iridescent green velvet. A considerable effort went into the construction of this bizarre feature yet its purpose remains elusive.

Despite being extensively investigated by curious Victorians, little evidence has been recovered from these passageways – and nothing that provides an unequivocal answer to the puzzle of what they were for. Used for defence they would have trapped their occupants with no means of escape and most are so damp inside that they would have offered poor storage for supplies.

That their purpose was ceremonial, rather than everyday, is indicated by one example at Carn Euny in Cornwall. In the south-west of Britain, such sites are called fogous – from the Cornish word for cave or underground chamber. Here, among the beautiful and eerie remains of an Iron Age village, is a component that adds an interesting slant to the issue. Entered via a portal, the first stage of this peculiar feature is a round room with a fireplace-like recess. This has been likened to a North American Indian sweat lodge and, if correct, places fogous and their Scottish counterparts firmly in the realms of the ritual. This fogou was the first stone structure in the village so clearly it was of great importance to Carn Euny's Iron Age inhabitants.

But arguably the most impressive of all the Cornish fogous is Halliggye. In shady woodland twelve miles east of Penzance, a key-shaped entrance leads into a labyrinthine maze of underground tunnels and chambers. Although Victorians reconstructed the entrance, the fogou itself dates back to the centuries just before the arrival of the Romans in Britain. Again, at Halliggye, there is no practical explanation for the tunnels, so an alternative theory for their construction is sought.

The maze was an early symbol associated with the cycles of rebirth. Interestingly, at Culsh, two cup-marks were found carved into the wall – possible symbols of female sexuality. When this souterrain was no longer required it was not simply abandoned. Instead, the tunnel was carefully filled with rich, dark earth – an act of ceremonial closure. These passages, it seems, were the work of ancient fertility cults seeking to ensure the survival of their tribe through the nurturing wombs of Mother Earth. Although they represented an impressive investment of labour, the sexuality of the earth, it will be seen, could also be indulged on a far greater scale.

From the Derrynasaggart hills of County Kerry rise the unmistakable outlines of the Paps of Anu.

CHAPTER FOUR

The Goddess Landscape

AT THE KING'S URGING, CÚCHULAIN COURTED EMER. DURING THEIR FIRST MEETING THEY SPOKE OF SEX FREELY AND EASILY. GLANCING AT EMER'S BREASTS, CÚCHULAIN SAID, 'I SEE A SWEET COUNTRY. I COULD REST MY WEAPON HERE.'

PETER CHERICI

Before the Romans arrived in Britain, an intimate relationship existed between the native people and their surroundings. Everything had a spirit. Oak trees, rocks and waterfalls possessed a life force that was intimately entwined with a landscape that was not 'it' but 'She'. The Great Earth Mother was omnipresent and the undulating, life-supporting land was her body. Hills were the breasts of the goddess, clefts between them were her cleavage, deep valleys and ravines were her vulvae, and the springs and rivers were revered as the sacred life force that flowed from her uterus. She was known by many names. In Ireland she was the goddess Anu or Anann and for many centuries Ireland itself was called the Land of Annan.

But the prehistoric world could be an inhospitable place. The land had not yet been tamed and survival was by no means assured against the elements, lack of food or vast virgin forests where wild animals roamed. Perhaps it is understandable that people seeking explanations about the world they inhabited saw familiar human forms in the landscape. The awe inspired by sacred places – where the body of the goddess was recognised in the natural topography – is still evident today in their enduring names.

On the border between the Irish counties of Cork and Kerry, two distinctive mountains stand out from the Derrynasaggart range of hills. The Paps – or breasts – of Anu are outrageously suggestive peaks protruding above the horizon. Known also as Da

Beautiful structures of overlapping stone complete the visual analogy of the Paps of Anu with the breasts of Ireland's mother goddess.

Chich Anann, the hills are named after the Mother Goddess of the mythological Tuatha Dé Danann, a divine and ancient tribe who, according to legend, once ruled Ireland. The word 'pap' probably originated from the Scandinavian for 'nipple' and these twin peaks are, indeed, strikingly breast-shaped.

Small farms nestle against the base of the nurturing slopes from where a steep walk to the top of either peak is rewarded with remarkable views of the surrounding landscape. Up here, the goddess is almost perfectly symmetrical, with one pap only four metres higher than the other. On a clear day the unmistakable outline of the Paps can be seen from almost sixty miles away and it is perhaps from a distance that the benefits of a little augmentation can best be appreciated. At the summit of each peak is a drystone-walled cairn, probably built some time in the later Neolithic period. In themselves, these are truly beautiful structures of overlapping stone but their real worth is in completing the visual analogy of the hills with the breasts of Ireland's Mother Goddess.

The association of the life-supporting land with the bodies of deities is by no means restricted to Ireland. Britain, north of Hadrian's Wall, seems to be particularly well endowed with suggestive twin peaks and Scotland's prehistoric folk certainly had an eye for appreciating the landscape's finer form. The islands of Islay and Jura lie off the intricately convoluted west coast of Scotland, part of the archipelago of the Inner Hebrides. Today the islands are perhaps most famous for their fine malt whiskeys but their particular significance for the ancient inhabitants of these parts lay in the distinctive topography of Jura.

Three mountains on the southern tip of the island with wonderfully-sounding names have even more evocative outlines. The hill in north of the group, known as Beinn an Oir or the Mountain of Gold rises steeply to a height of 785 metres above sea level. To the west the rounded summit of Beinn A'Chaolais, the Mountain of Sound, lies just fifty metres below its

sister, while in the south-east Beinn Shiantaidh, the Sacred Mountain, is considerably smaller. The shapes of all three hills change dramatically depending upon the viewpoint. Collectively they are known as the Paps of Jura and, when seen from the nearby island of Islay, Beinn Shiantaidh is completely hidden from view behind the other two remarkably breast-shaped hills.

Of course, it cannot be assumed that five thousand years ago people anthropomorphised the horizon as people invariably do today. But in the landscape of north-eastern Islay, these ubiquitous peaks dominate the skyline in a way that cannot be ignored. Their name alone suggests that for centuries the people of the Inner Hebrides have interpreted their mammary presence in this way, underlined by the fact that many of the island's ancient standing stones were placed with reference to the Paps.

Not far from the tiny harbour village of Port Askaig is an area of high boggy grassland known as Mullach Dubh. Here, among the sheep and tall, tussocky grass, and with a clear sight line north-eastward to the Paps, stands a single squat block of oolitic stone. A reference to the breast-shaped hills was clearly intended in the erection of this stone as the profile of its top mirrors exactly the outline of Beinn A'Chaolais and from here the midsummer sun would have risen directly over the Paps. Although standing stones have been seen as generic tokens of masculinity,

The Paps of Anu: small farms nestle against the nurturing slopes of the hills.

The Paps of Jura off Scotland's west coast dominate an otherwise low-lying horizon.

researchers have described the Mullach Dubh stone as having 'a naturally formed vulva-shaped opening' which they felt was significant. Perhaps the stone to be placed in such intimate association with the breasts of the goddess was carefully selected for its natural feminine properties.

The nurturing presence of Beinn A' Chaolais, Beinn an Oir and Beinn Shiantaidh was evidently of fundamental importance to early communities on Islay and Jura. Their influence resonated through the monuments and actions of the islanders and perhaps even beyond, on a clear day, to those living within sight of the hills on the mainland. Ancient tradition, upheld by the Lord of the Isles until at least the sixteenth century, required them to be venerated accordingly. Today the mountains still exude a strangely formidable presence and, over much of the islands, their maternal grey form is a constant reminder of those customs.

Elsewhere in Scotland, it seems, people also saw the female anatomy in the outlines of the mountains, but breast-shaped hills did not have to come in pairs. At the head of Glencoe, where the rough, moorland grass rises to a pointed, rocky peak, is another hill known as the Pap. The Maiden Paps in Bearsden, just west of Glasgow, and the Maiden Paps in the Borders near Hermitage Castle are smaller, perkier hills whose assets, similarly, did not go unappreciated by the early inhabitants of these regions. Qualitative analysis was undertaken at Lochnagar where we find Chioch Mor and Chioch Bheag, the Big Breast and the Little Breast, and near Loch Nevis, with Garbh Chioch Mhor, the Big Rough Breast, and Garbh Chioch Bheag, the Little Rough Breast. Other place names hint at associations between either the appearance of a hill or perhaps activities that traditionally took place there. On Ben Alligin in Torridon is a hill known as Tom na Grugaich or the Maidens' Hillock, and in the Cuillin range of mountains on the Isle of Skye the more intrepid may come across Sgurr nan Gilean — the Peak of the Young

Mullach Dubh standing stone on Islay mirrors the distant outline of the Paps of Jura.

Men. At A Chioch in the Cairngorms they were satisfied with simply the Breast.

Prehistoric communities also recognised the Earth Mother in two wonderful mountains just north-west of Aberdeen. Mither Tap, or Mother Tit lies at the eastern end of the dark massif of the Bennachie hills, a hugely conical sacred mountain. Her equivalent can be found sixteen miles to the north-west in Tap O'Noth, the Northern Tit, a brooding recumbent hill that dominates the surrounding land like the skyline figure of Cailleach na Mòintich on the Isle of Lewis.

As on Islay, the familiar profile of these hills seems ever present on the horizon, their ubiquitous outlines forming the backdrop to every view. The granite and feldspar tors of Mither Tap and Tap O'Noth define the east and west extents of a sacred landscape where, four and a half thousand years ago, stone circle mania gripped the people of this area. Perhaps inspired by the sheer natural beauty of this lush and fertile region, they erected a profusion of carefully sited standing stones and magnificent recumbent stone rings. Many of these seem to have been carefully erected with clear views to either of the breast-shaped hills, suggesting that the presence of their landscape form was a main consideration to these prehistoric architects.

Over 350 miles further south, midway between the cities of Manchester and Sheffield, the gritty bulk of Mam Tor was once holding the prehistoric inhabitants of the High Peak in similar awe. Literally translated, its name means 'Heights of the Mother' and this rugged mass, the greatest sacred hill in Derbyshire, reaches an altitude of over 500 metres. Rarely without a heavy blanket of snow during the winter months, Mam Tor affords spectacular views of the Hope and Edale valleys, and the stunning geological shelf of Kinder Scout.

Although not overtly bosomy in profile, this mountain clearly had connections with a fecund earth goddess. The Roman goddess Matrona was an ancient deity of motherhood. In Britain Madron was the Mother of All. She represented the bountiful Waters of Life and was closely associated with springs and sacred wells. And there are tales that a freshwater stream known as Odin's Sitch issued from the summit of the nurturing hill.

But perhaps it is unwise to limit our view of the goddess to the standard twin peaks of the human female. A formidable hill near Lochnagar in Scotland is called Beinn Cichean, or Mountain of the Teats. This ancient naming may be a reminder that the goddess spirit dwelt in everything and that the fertility of animals was central to the well-being of these early farmers. It could also be suggestive of a belief in more exotic deities similar to the Eastern goddess Artemis, known in Ephesus as Dea Anna – the many breasted

The rugged mass of Mam Tor, or Heights of the Mother, is the greatest sacred hill in Derbyshire.

patroness of fertility and nursing. She had strong connections to the Central America goddess, Mayahuel, whose name meant the 'Woman with Four Hundred Breasts'. Clearly, when it comes to fertility, quantity counts.

With the successful adoption of new farming methods the population continued to increase throughout the first millennium BC. The Iron Age climate, though, was inconveniently worsening and from around 600 BC, fortified settlements occupying

The female appearance of Yeavering Bell was emphasised in the Iron Age by the enclosure of the twin peaks in a loose figure-of-eight stone wall.

defendable hilltop sites began to appear. These hillforts with their encircling ramparts, walls and ditches were clearly the response to a growing competition for land and resources that, at times, led inevitably to conflict. Evidence has been recovered from some hillforts of intensive and highly organised occupation, but this was not necessarily the case.

Some seem to have been used only intermittently in times of threat or as venues for occasional communal gatherings. This introduces an element of use that was ritual rather than purely defensive. When faced with a choice of suitable hills on which to construct these elevated enclosures, sites were often chosen on a double-peaked hilltop. Is it possible that these ceremonial centres which also offered safe retreat were deliberately built on hills that were identified with the nurturing breasts of mother earth?

The Northumbrian Cheviots are a stunningly desolate range of hills where the occasional wild goat can still be seen. The northern end of the massif sweeps down to Milfield Plain, a wide expanse of flat land where traces of ancient trackway and settlement survive. One of the last bracken-covered hills before high ground gives way to low is Yeavering Bell, whose sides rise up, draped in a tapestry of earthy russets and greens, to a magnificently rounded double summit. A climb to the top is rewarded with incredible views as far north as the River Tweed and eastward to the hazy blue line of the distant North Sea.

The route up invariably crosses a tumbled rubble of rocks that encloses the twin peaks in a loose figure of eight, the remnants of a stone wall that once tapered up from a base over three metres wide. Inside the enclosure the remains of 130 wooden huts were found, evidence that people from the valleys and the plain once seasonally occupied this lofty place. A room with a view, it seems, is not an entirely modern requirement. But why build such a distinctively shaped enclosure on Yeavering Bell when there are other equally defendable hills nearby? To prehistoric farmers this hill would have presented a blatant reference to the body of the mother earth. If her presence was

recognised in the natural lines of Yeavering Bell then it made an obvious site for ceremonial gatherings. It may have been to enhance this comparison that a small domed cairn, similar to those on the Paps of Anu, was added to the eastern summit.

For thousands of years across geographically diverse cultures the maze design was a deeply symbolic motif. Such patterns appear in a third millennium BC rock engraving in Italy, on an Etruscan vase dating from the seventh century BC and on a pillar in Roman Pompeii. Near Tintagel in Cornwall a footpath winds steeply down a lush and overgrown ravine to sea level. At a spot known as Rocky Valley, where a small tributary widens to meet the Atlantic Ocean, the vertical cliff is carved with the delicately scratched engravings of prehistoric artists. Two delicate designs spread across the rock face in a pattern whose stylistic elements have been compared to other maze depictions. The most common interpretation of these labyrinthine motifs is that of the soul's journey through life, death and rebirth. Such a symbol of regeneration was powerfully ? with elements of sexual energy seen in the related image of the coiled serpent.

Nearly one hundred miles away, in the county of Somerset, the soft green hill of Glastonbury Tor, with the instantly recognisable silhouette of its tower, can be seen from a great distance rising from the

An ancient terraced route winds around the slopes of Glastonbury Tor.

At Rocky Valley in Cornwall, two delicate maze designs spread across the vertical rock face.

Summerland meadows. The name's derivation is complex but it is thought, at one stage, to have been Ynis Witrin, or Isle of Glass. This natural knoll lies in an area of otherwise flat ground which, in winter, was too flooded to inhabit, and even today, when a blanket of dawn mist covers the Somerset Levels the Tor still seems to rise as though from encircling waters.

Glastonbury Tor is also surrounded by perhaps more myths and legends than any other hill in Britain. Viewed from one direction, the horizon is said to be evocative of a female recumbent figure, with the profile of the Glastonbury Tor forming the left breast. The Tor is also reputed to be hollow – with a series of springs forming a network of subterranean waterways beneath its slopes – and the dwelling place of faeries. It is not surprising that prehistoric people, who saw a divine spirit in the landscape, were aware of this place.

The presence of ancient visitors on this sacred hill is betrayed by what they left behind. A few scattered flints that could easily have been dropped by accident tell us nothing of their beliefs about the Tor. The discovery here of a precious ceremonial greenstone axe, a symbol of fecundity used in fertility rituals, suggests, however, that even five thousand years ago this hill was a focus for goddess worship. Around the slopes of the Tor a terraced pathway winds its way up in an ancient backtracking route that is now faint and worn. Although only clearly discernable along the north face, the path loops around the Tor on seven ascending levels in a labyrinthine pattern reminiscent of the design on ancient Cretan coins. Striking similarities have also been noted with the iconographic representation of Mother Earth by North American Hopi Indians, with spirals seen on the breasts of early European goddess images and on the walls of Newgrange tomb. This path, it seems, was originally designed to encircle the breast of the recumbent goddess of the land.

One of the many legends surrounding Glastonbury Tor tells of an ancient stone temple on its summit. In the tenth or eleventh century the top of the hill was levelled in preparation for erecting a large church. As at Llanbrynmair in Powys, this attempt to physically replace the sacred pagan site with a centre for Christian worship only served to strengthen the visual comparison of these hills to breasts. No doubt to the satisfaction of any remaining local pagans, the Tor's church was destroyed by an earthquake in September 1275. Until recently it was thought that all pre-Christian archaeological evidence on the Tor had been obliterated in the Middle Ages but in February 2002 an excavation by the Glastonbury Antiquarian Society uncovered what was interpreted as the foundations of a circular stone structure. It is tempting to wonder whether these were the remains of an ancient fertility temple, a ceremonial centre at the heart of the maze.

The alterations made to natural hills for the purpose of enhancing their sexual aspects are undeniably impressive, but in the grounds of Marlborough College in Wiltshire is evidence that work was done by devotees of a goddess fertility cult that bordered on the obsessive.

Marlborough Mound, or Merlin's Mount as it is also known, is an artificial steep-sided, tree-covered mound that rises behind the rosy stone of historic college buildings. It was thought by some to have been constructed as part of a medieval castle but two excavated finds suggest that its origins may lie much further back in time. Roman coins discovered in the mound in the seventeenth century could, conceivably,

The symbolism behind Silbury Hill is complex and manyfold.

have found their way into the fabric of a Norman motte. But when red deer antlers of a type used as picks by prehistoric builders were uncovered deep inside the hill during excavations in 1912, it seemed the date of the mound was being pushed back into prehistory.

In the early eighteenth century it was transformed into a spiral-clad garden feature in the grounds of a house built for Lord Hertford. Perhaps this remodelling rekindled the spiralled fertility symbolism intended by the mound's prehistoric creators. As intriguing as Marlborough Mound is, though, maybe it was only a practice run for the construction of a much larger monument less than five miles to the west along the course of the River Kennet.

Silbury Hill, a broad conical mass near the great stone circle of Avebury, rises from the heart of the Marlborough Downs like a gigantic upturned pudding basin. The largest artificial mound in Europe, it is also one of the most awe-inspiring and enigmatic earthworks in Britain.

The construction of Silbury Hill was an engineering feat to rival the building of the Great Pyramids at around the same time – about four thousand years ago – in the desert outside Cairo. Covering an area of over two hectares, it contains over 250,000 cubic metres of clay and chalk and it is estimated that the work, using deer-antler picks and ox-bone shovels, must have taken more than eighteen million work hours to complete. Centuries later, legends had brewed of a great burial and treasure that was thought to lie at the heart of the mound. In October 1776 a team of Cornish miners from Mendip led by the Duke of Northumberland excavated a shaft all the way from the top of the mound to ground level. This opening up of Silbury Hill began in a blaze of publicity but they ended up finding nothing. So what compelled prehistoric farmers to undertake such a Herculean – and seemingly pointless – task?

Hazel twigs and fragments of deer antler found inside the hill have been radiocarbon-dated to the Late Neolithic period, around 2400 BC. Although it is not known exactly in which year work began on Silbury Hill, perversely, from the inclusion of tiny winged ants in the lowest layers, archaeologists are sure that the very first shovelfuls of soil were thrown in place during late July or early August. The image of goddess-obsessed people toiling in the heat of the midsummer sun and pestered by a profusion of airborne ants brings the past poignantly into focus.

Silbury was built in three distinct phases, each one grander in design than the last. It began as a small mound of gravel, soil and turf, kept in place by a ring of wooden stakes. This had not been in place long when, it seems, the decision was taken to enlarge this modest feature. A ditch was dug some distance from the stakes and the excavated chalk rubble was heaved into the middle around a complex structure of reinforced partitions that completely obscured the original mound. But the first two phases diminish in comparison to the final, and most architecturally ambitious, structure. Another hectare of ground and all traces of the earlier designs were subsumed beneath a colossal mountain of chalk that towers nearly forty metres above the ground.

Numerous eminent archaeologists have excavated the mound since the Duke of Northumberland's first

Silbury Hill, rising from its boggy bed, emulates the first piece of land to rise from the chaos of primeval watery creation.

exploration in 1776. Legend still maintained that the hill was the resting-place of King Sel and that life-size figures in gold of the king and his horse lay buried beneath it. In 1922 the famous Egyptologist, Sir Flinders Petrie, attempted to find an entrance to the burial chamber which all antiquarians believed lay at the heart of the mound. After he, too, was frustrated it was realised that it was not what lay beneath but rather the mound itself that was important.

As the result of a series of archaeological excavations in the latter half of the twentieth century, it was agreed that Silbury Hill was constructed like a

95

giant, tiered wedding cake with consecutively smaller drums of chalk rubble rising up through its core. In the summer of 2000 archaeologists re-surveyed the mound using seismic equipment and a satellite guided global positioning system. The finely detailed digital model of the hill created from this data indicates that the hill was subtly faceted and rose, not in simple incremental terraces, but in a continuous ascending spiral. The implications of this are profound. Silbury Hill, it seems, had a navigable processional route to the top. Modern archaeologists, instead of plundering its depths in search of the mythical burial treasure of some ancient warlord, now focus on trying to understand the meaning and symbolism behind the mystery of Silbury Hill. What may be most important is the spiralling shape that draped and enfolded the entire surface of the mound and provided a ceremonial path to the summit of Silbury Hill.

The location of Silbury is curious. Built on a low natural terrace on the floor of the valley and surrounded by rolling chalk downs it can only be seen from relatively close by. This suggests that the hill was not built as a beacon or proud display of territory. A silken covering of grass now rustles gently across its slopes on a breezy day but, when first constructed, the bare white chalk of Silbury Hill would have shone like milky flesh. Considered within the context of the wider ceremonial landscape of Avebury,

interpretations now revolve around a symbolic fertile earth goddess.

The valley floor here is not much higher than the natural water table and Silbury Hill was sited at a point where natural springs emerge from between two layers of chalk. The excavation of a broad, pan-shaped ditch around the hill not only provided material for the construction of the mound but also ensured that, for much of the year, a shallow pool of water surrounded Silbury Hill.

In many cultures the earth is believed to have first risen from the watery floor of the universe. Ancient Greek philosophers maintained that the earth not only originated from, but also consisted of and returned to, the water on which it floated. The image of the world floating on water is one that endured for centuries, to be encapsulated even in later garden design. Prehistoric people would have been intimately aware that new life grew in the swollen bellies of females and arrived along a birth passage, heralded by a swoosh of liquid. The most compelling explanation for the imagery in play at Silbury is that the mound was intended to represent the swollen, pregnant belly of a great female deity. The pan-shaped trench was her womb and the water within it was a metaphor for the miraculous and sacred amniotic fluid, the water of life, which brought all new creations into the world. It is possible that Silbury Hill, rising out of its boggy

Swallowhead Spring near Avebury – the points where water issued from the body of the earth were particularly sacred.

bed, was intended to emulate the first piece of land to rise from the chaos of primeval watery creation, the very body of the Mother Earth itself.

Of course, to modern people the hill has represented various aspects of an earth goddess. Silbury has also been seen as a nurturing, life-giving breast, and

as an omphalos – an enormous navel at the spiritual centre of the universe. These interpretations are certainly valid: indeed the symbolism employed at Silbury may be complex and manyfold. The hill may well have been built on a site that was already regarded as sacred in the natural landscape. Some places held enormous power for prehistoric people and, in this area of life-giving springs, an open-air shrine probably preceded the construction of the hill. After its completion, Silbury would certainly have been steeped in magic and ritual. Imitation or enhancement of the natural landscape goddess was perceived to be essential and these sites became a focus for participation in the earth's reproductive cycles – a ceremonial stage for encouraging her continued fertility.

The precise choice of location for the construction of Silbury also seems to have been made with distinct reference to another important water source. The Swallowhead Spring, source of the sacred River Kennet, lies less than half a mile south of Silbury Hill. It was a focal point of the landscape and its relevance could be seen as late as the eighteenth century in a harvest fertility ritual when water collected from the Swallowhead Spring was brought to the summit of the hill.

It is a phenomenon of the Swallowhead Spring that every year in November it ceases to flow. The summer-long evaporation of water from the chalklands reduces the subterranean water table to a level where water no longer flows from the otherwise reliable spring. The River Kennet, which at other times of the year supports whole ecosystems of plants and animals, completely dries up. Only after two months of heavy winter precipitation does the water

level rise sufficiently for the spring to flow once more. The scarcity of water experienced in the meantime was reflected in the old proverb 'Between Martinmas and Yule, water's worth wine in any pule'. Little wonder, then, that early farmers revered this source of water when they were reminded so regularly of the barrenness brought by its disappearance.

The ritual significance of water to prehistoric people cannot be overstated. Rivers and streams were literally of cosmic importance and the points where they issued from or returned into the body of the Mother Earth were particularly sacred. Perhaps because of their orientation towards the rising sun, east-flowing rivers, such as the Thames and the Witham, were favourite choices for bestowing votive offerings. The connection between water and fecundity was a strong one. Water, as embodied in the goddess Madron, was the bringer of all life; in Ireland and Wales the shape-shifting god of the sea, Manannan Mac Lir, was also the god of rebirth. A belief in the power of certain springs to cure ailments, especially infertility, is one that persisted widely until the last century.

The strength of the association between a fertile goddess of the land and the water that irrigates it is demonstrated by the survival, from pre-Christian times, of names connecting the two. In the south-west of the island of Islay is a plateau of high ground – a place of cattle grazing amongst the heather and of dark, sodden peat bogs. Here, not far inland from Kilchiaran Bay is Loch Conailbhe, Lake of the Goddess. Undoubtedly a sacred place in ancient times, this loch, lying equidistant between two great standing stones the alignment of which points in the direction of the Paps of Jura, may also have been a venue for water-based fertility rites.

The Paps of Anu in Ireland also have an intimate link with water. The northern sides of the hills are much steeper than those to the south but the perilous cliffs between the hills do give way to lower, peat-covered slopes. Here, in the cleavage between the two Paps, is a teardrop-shaped lake known as Lough Nageeha. A lake in this auspicious position, nestled between the breasts of the goddess, would undoubtedly have been regarded as sacred by the prehistoric inhabitants of the area. Sure enough, not far from the shores of the lake were found the remains of small circular huts probably linked to ritual activity at the sacred waters of Lough Nageeha.

Many stone circles throughout Britain and Ireland, already recognised as sites where the natural forces or spirits were invoked, also had connections to water that were more than coincidental. Some rings were physically joined to water by lines of earth or stone as at Stonehenge, where an avenue curved its way

towards the River Avon. Occasionally, though, the sacred elements of water and circle were combined in one potent setting.

In Kilmartin Glen in Argyll, home of one of Scotland's richest concentrations of prehistoric ritual monuments, a unique site was recently discovered by archaeologists. On a broad terrace with magnificent views across the fertile valley, the remains were

The sacred waters of Lough Nageeha lie in the cleavage between the Paps of Anu.

Le Pinacle on Jersey's north-west coast has been recognised since prehistoric times as a natural manifestation of male sexuality.

uncovered of a vast timber circle. Here, thirty oak tree trunks, some nearly half a metre in diameter, were set in a ring. Alongside were the cist burials of six early Bronze Age individuals, including a young woman, buried with a beautifully decorated ceramic pot. Within the timber circle archaeologists found traces of an inner ring of posts. Like totem poles, these posts surrounded a large, deep hollow – a votive pool at the heart of this sacred site. Posts also lined a processional avenue leading to the pool where, it is believed, offerings were made to the deities of the fertile earth and water.

But sites like Kilmartin are rare. They provide a tantalising glimpse of the wider occurrence of rituals and fertility rites that would have taken place in pre-Christian Britain and Ireland between two and five thousand years ago. The evidence has been recognised at just a handful of places but the earth goddess, in all her natural and fertile splendour, must have been acknowledged in wooded glades and on hillsides throughout the land.

The favours of a potent sexual deity were also apparently sought while travelling through the landscape. A figurine discovered buried beside the Bell Trackway, an ancient boardwalk constructed across the marshy ground of the Somerset Levels, had been carved from the wood of the ash tree. Well endowed both with pronounced breasts and an extended phallus, this hermaphroditic figure seems to have been placed upside down in the mud beside the track around 3000 BC. Its purpose, it seems, was as a votive offering – perhaps to ensure the successful construction of the pathway and the safe passage of travellers.

Traces of a causeway have also been recently discovered leading from an ancient settlement near Sedbergh in the Howgill Hills of south-east Cumbria. The pathway leads mysteriously up a narrow ravine to the spray-shrouded plunge pool of a roaring waterfall, Cautley Spout. The pool, an unlikely source of fresh drinking water for the settlement, was of sufficient importance to the people of this ancient village to warrant the construction of a formal path. We can only guess at whether ceremonies took place at Cautley Spout but it is tempting to think that the hills have rendered up secrets of one more sacred place where the natural union of sex and the landscape may have been worshipped.

This natural union can also be witnessed at the southernmost end of the British Isles, on the island of Jersey. Here, above the craggy shore where breaking Atlantic waves incessantly pound the rocks in a spray-drenched and deafening display of power, a single massive pillar of rock towers above the coast. The tapering form of Le Pinacle is immediately striking to modern visitors as one of nature's contributions to the wealth of stone phalluses but, more importantly, this rocky column has been recognised by people as exactly that for thousands of years.

Le Pinacle appears to have been the focus of attention of a Channel Island fertility cult and is proof that it was not only a female goddess whose form was seen in the natural landscape. Long before the arrival of the Romans in Britain, stones were being brought to this spectacular place and carefully placed to form enclosures that encircled the phallic rock. This act not only acknowledged, but also emphasised the geological erection, and the use of this as a ritual site

A single humpbacked boulder that rises from the grass at Cairnbaan glistens when wet like the highly decorated surface of a burnished bronze shield.

from Neolithic to Roman times clearly demonstrates the enduring attraction of this naturally sexual form.

Black Elk of the North American Oglala Sioux maintained: 'Everything the power of the world does is done in a circle. . . . The sun comes forth and goes down again in a circle. The moon does the same, and both are round. Even the seasons form a great circle in their changing, and always come back again to where they were. The life of a man is a circle to childhood and so it is in everything where power moves.'

Hiking through open parts of upland Britain, people today may be surprised to come across earthfast stone slabs that at first glance appear pock-marked and channelled by a lifetime's exposure to wind and rain. Closer examination reveals some of the hollows and grooves to be not the result of natural erosion but a mass of intricately carved circles, cups and lines, covering entire surfaces of outcropping rock with the complex and abstract designs of prehistoric rock art.

Magical and enduring, this ancient form of engraved art is known by the collective term of cup-and-ring markings. Carved into bare rock by picking insistently and delicately with a hard stone chisel, the patterns include seemingly endless variations of swirls, spirals, dots and lines but the name reflects the overwhelming occurrence of small dished hollows or cups. These cups are often surrounded by one or more concentric rings that expand like ripples on a pond up to two feet in diameter.

Because the carvings are found in isolated places and have been smoothed by exposure to the elements their existence went entirely unnoticed until the middle of the nineteenth century. Since then, many elaborate explanations have been proffered for these enigmatic markings which have been interpreted variously as knife-sharpening holes, adders' nests and the 'shop windows' of prehistoric tattoo artists.

In the hills two miles north of the waters of Loch Fyne is a concentration of Argyll's most impressive

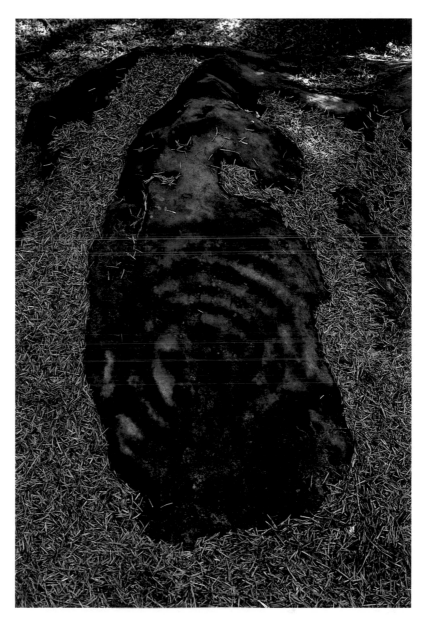

Buttony in Northumberland encapsulates the other-worldliness of ancient cup-and-ring markings.

Weetwood Moor hosts some of the most dramatic rock art in Britain.

expanses of cup-and-ring-marked stones. On the gentle south-east-facing slopes of Cnoc na Moine, two sets of carvings can be seen at a site known as Cairnbaan. The walk to reach the higher stone is rewarded with a compact and well-defined group of cup marks covering a single humpbacked boulder that rises from the grass. When the sky is laden with heavy cloud these marks seem dull and worn with age but as sunlight catches the surface of this stone when wet, it glistens like the highly decorated face of a burnished bronze shield.

The dramatic location of many of the carved slabs within the landscape, on hill tops and cliff edges overlooking broad valleys, would seem to suggest that the place itself was important. Perhaps with each successive visit and carving, these rocky outcrops accumulated sacredness and became places where early people communicated with the powers of creation. Clearly, these abstract designs do not depict straightforward, everyday objects, and their meaning, hidden in a language of symbolism remains elusive.

One idea, although it sounds more like a riddle, is that the answer to the cup-and-ring marks essentially lies within the problem. It is not surprising that this language of hieroglyphs cannot readily be understood if these motifs were communicating concepts or values too sacred for depiction by ordinary imagery. Stylistically similar passage-grave art appears

A dizzying array of prehistoric art covers the vertical cliffs of Scotland's Ballochmyle Walls.

extensively in the chambered prehistoric burial tombs of Ireland and northern Wales, giving support to the widely accepted notion that these swirling, circular patterns are deeply ritual in nature. Such designs are thought by some to be symbolic of fertility through the renewal of life after death, an entreaty to a mother goddess for enriched fruitfulness, elicited through

ancestors who have returned to the body of her earth. Could a similar explanation be extended to these mysterious cup-and-ring marks?

Weetwood Moor is a beautiful and lonely expanse of high, heathery ground just a few miles east of the small town of Wooler in Northumberland. Sheep-grazed pastures, edged by lichen-encrusted drystone

A spiral flows into concentric rings at Little Meg in Cumbria.

walls, give way to tall, dark-green plumes of coniferous plantation before the land rises and opens on to the moor. With some suddenness, rocks appear underfoot, marvellously engraved with the enigmatic motifs of this area's prehistoric inhabitants.

Still wet from an overnight drenching, the stone slabs are tinged with hues of pink in the gentle light just after dawn. Shallow lines radiate from nearly all the sets of rings, interconnecting the circles in a flowing design that glints with shallow pools of rainwater. These elaborately carved rocks, hosting a series of neatly pecked cup marks surrounded by some of the preserved concentric rings in Britain, lay undiscovered until the mid-nineteenth century.

Cup-and-ring markings, despite their geographical diversity, display a remarkable degree of consistency. The central cup appears to be a fundamental component and this may provide a clue to their meaning. Prehistoric cave art in Scandinavia and in northern Italy includes depictions of humans that can be identified, variously, as males and females. Some of the males proudly sport erections while groups of females are shown with cup marks between their legs. These, too, are reminiscent of the cup carved blocks found alongside chalk phalluses at Windmill Hill in Wiltshire. It would seem that these ancient motifs were widely recognised as symbolic of female sexuality.

In 1986, a man walking his dog in the Ayr Valley discovered one of the most spectacular prehistoric rock art sites in the British Isles. At Ballochmyle, a path surreally descends into a gorge reminiscent of the Land that Time Forgot. Towering cliffs of vibrant red sandstone are draped in primeval creepers and ferns, and a stream gushes along the shady depths interrupted by deep pools. Here, a vast wall of ancient rock art almost twenty metres in length was revealed, displaying a bewildering array of designs in an enormous mural of spirals, sun-wheels, cup marks and circles.

This inaccessible gorge would not have been chosen as a convenient location for an open-air gallery in which local artists could promote their handiwork. It seems more likely that the gorge itself inspired the rock art. Anyone stumbling unsuspectingly into this rain forest time capsule would be convinced that what was being celebrated here was the lush fertility of nature at its very best.

Detailed studies of the intricate dimensions of these patterns have suggested a connection in both proportion and design with the infinitely larger megalithic stone circles. That carvings are actually found on the stones of megalithic circles strengthens this association. In Cumbria, Little Meg, a tiny ruined kerb-circle, lies just half a mile from the giant stone ring of Long Meg and her Daughters. A recumbent slab lies next to the tallest of Little Meg's stones and on this are carved a magnificent spiral and concentric rings. This is not the most elaborate or the most deeply incised of British carvings. There is an elegant beauty, though, in the simplicity of the design as the curve of the spiral flows into the outer ring of the nested circles. Encapsulated within a single stone, it seems, are the beliefs and aspirations of many generations – their reliance on the natural cycles of a landscape and their artistic, votive offering upon it.

Bath's Roman baths: accounts testify that, on occasions, the authorities had to be called in to restore decency at bath-houses.

CHAPTER FIVE

When in Rome . . .

WAS IT IN SECRET THAT YOU CARVED, AS CURLEWS CRIED,
AND FINGERS ACHED TO SCULPT YOUR SHAPE IN STONE?
WHAT HIDDEN YEARNINGS FILLED YOUR MIND,
AS THE PHALLUS FORMED BENEATH YOUR HAND?

GWEN JACOBSON

In AD 43, the Emperor Claudius was at the helm of the greatest empire the world had ever seen, stretching from Portugal in the west to Syria in the east and across the Mediterranean as far south as Africa. But a tribe in Britain, known as the Catuvellauni, presented a potentially hostile force on the northern frontier of the Empire — a situation that was unacceptable to this ambitious ruler. With this in mind (and possibly seduced by the idea of expanding Rome's territory still further), Claudius launched a full-scale invasion from the continent. After landing unopposed on the shores of Kent, an army of four legions made their way inland. Within days they had crossed the river Thames and forcibly occupied the Catuvellaunian capital at Colchester. The Roman era in Britain had begun.

But as the soldiers of the Roman army engaged in combat against the warriors of the British tribes, the clashes were not only between the continental gladius and the native broadsword, but also between two vastly different cultures. The Celtic world they had invaded was an animistic one. Spirits dwelt in rocks and oak trees and a fertile mother goddess was omnipresent in the streams and hillsides of the landscape. Women were intimately connected to the fruitful earth and their sexuality was entwined with the renewal of all life. The gods of the sun and of the sky were the deified embodiment of the male psyche and the two existed in natural complement to one another coming together through divine sexual union. Powers greater than human encouraged

copulation for pleasure and demanded it for ceremony.

One of the most striking cultural differences between natives and the continental arrivals lay in the respective roles of men and women. Roman society was heavily patriarchal. Women, barred from holding any form of office, ranked barely higher than slaves and could only achieve any degree of status through bearing their husband's children – preferably boys. It may be going too far to suggest that Celtic society was egalitarian, but women of the British tribes certainly enjoyed a high degree of freedom. Celtic women controlled their own sexuality. They selected their own lovers and husbands, with the option of both if their needs were not fulfilled. A Celtic woman could 'divorce' her husband if he grew too fat, as this was seen as affecting his ability to satisfy her in the bedroom. Roman writers described the 'barbarian' tribes as promiscuous and unrestrained, remarking that they indulged in 'several categories of marriage'. Celtic women could hold religious office in the druidic order, could engage in politics and, as the Romans would soon find out, could bear arms.

In what is now East Anglia lived a tribe known as the Iceni and they were ruled by a woman – the legendary Queen Boudicca. For refusing to acquiesce to the invading horde she was publicly flogged and both her young daughters raped. Undeterred, in AD 60 Boudicca led the tribes of southern Britain in rebellion against the Romans. But the Celtic warriors were ultimately no match for the might of the imperial army and, rather than submit, Queen Boudicca committed suicide.

The Roman army advanced north and west quelling resistance when it was met. In their wake they left compliant native rulers and a developing, fragile peace. The worship of Celtic deities continued, unaffected at first by the influx of new beliefs from Rome. These incomers were, in fact, just as superstitious as the natives and, finding themselves in unfamiliar surroundings, were only too willing to placate the local gods by making the appropriate votive gestures.

A Romano-British settlement was established just south-east of Silbury Hill near Avebury. This choice of location so near to the gigantic mound and a wealth of Roman finds from it suggest that after the conquest this area remained a focus of activity. Perhaps, then, even this patriarchal force was moved to venerate the fertility aspect of the Great Earth Goddess.

Slowly, elements of the two cultures began to merge. A thin veneer of continental influence was gradually draped over the Celtic deities of the rivers and woods. Dea Nutrix, a Roman goddess of death and the afterlife, was eased in alongside Celtic figures such as Cerridwen and Blodeuwedd in continuation of

Coventina's Well was one of the most elaborate freshwater shrines in Roman Britain.

the connection between death, sex and regeneration. The Romans did not venerate a fertile Mother Earth as seen in the hills and valleys but they did acknowledge human motherhood. Every year on the first day of March, a festival was held – the Matronalia – in honour of married women. It commemorated the founding of a temple to Juno Lucina, goddess of childbirth, and also intimately associated with the moon. Votive stone carvings of goddesses were common in Roman Britain and a standard depiction on plaques was the 'Matres' or trinity of maternal goddesses. Benevolent providers, the Matres are sometimes shown bearing fruit and bread in a symbolic gesture that echoes the harvest festivals previously associated with pagan hills like Silbury. An element of the Celtic goddess in her triple form of mother, maiden and crone was, it seems, perpetuated by the Romans in their trinity of the Matres.

Sacred springs and streams – believed by the Celts to issue directly from the body of the earth goddess – also continued as places of worship after the invasion. Offerings were still being made at wells near Silbury Hill and the Marlborough Mound. In fact, the generative forces of some Roman deities adopted a native-style association with water sources. Just south of Hadrian's Wall in Northumberland, in an exposed landscape of sweeping views and big skies, is the site of a small shrine left by the Roman army. Coventina's Well at Carrawburgh is a natural spring – now just a small weedy pond – but the trickle of water between reeds can still be heard as it emerges from the ground and begins a journey down to the River Tyne. It was discovered in 1876 and when its contents were excavated, what at first looked like dumped rubbish turned out to be over thirteen thousand votive offerings. Bronze pins, brooches and coins from the reign of Antonius Pius had all been surrendered to the goddess of the spring in the hope of pleas being answered. People worshipping here were clearly of humble means since the coins and trinkets were not of

high value but the appeals for divine intervention were, no doubt, just as earnest as those of much wealthier devotees. Given the intimate and enduring association between water sources and fecundity, it is likely that many offerings at Coventina's Well were made for very personal reasons related to fertility, sex or marriage.

Confirmation of this connection has been uncovered from sites throughout the country in the form of exquisitely carved stone tablets. At High Rochester Roman camp, due north of Carrawburgh, a stone frieze was discovered depicting Venus, the goddess of love and beauty. She is revealed naked, bathing in a woodland spring attended by two water nymphs bearing a ewer and a shell basin. Although the tableau was found incorporated within a water tank it may have originally adorned a fountain. Celtic influences are also visible within the tablet's predominantly classical design. A male head and two phalluses appear above the watery maidens, and in Celtic iconography the head and the phallus were the most potent sexual symbols and sources of fertility. Interestingly, the subjects of this scene, reflected in the erotic artwork at Pompeii, were adopted centuries later as a generic brothel sign in Renaissance Italy.

Although Venus was among the many continental deities brought to Britain after the invasion, native deities were also willingly embraced by the Romans. At Caerleon in Newport a tile was found on which

Over two million litres of hot water flow daily into the Roman baths at Bath.

was depicted the goddess Sul, or Sulis. In a scene called 'Aquae Sulis' or 'Goddess Sul Bathing' this local deity of hot springs rises from a fountain which also graphically forms her vulva. As though underlining her reproductive energy and life force, Sul is escorted by two dolphins – animals that were symbolic of fertility.

Shrines at freshwater springs, known as nymphaea, became popular throughout Roman Britain. At the Chedworth villa in Gloucester and Housesteads fort in Northumberland basins were installed where the spring issued from the ground. Shrines were added with sculptures of naked water nymphs and the ritually

113

The high vaulted ceiling at Bath's Roman bath-house has long since fallen in and the main pool is now roofed by the sky.

imbued water was piped around the buildings in an early but effective running supply. And at Lullingstone in Kent an underground room was uncovered which, it is believed, was the scene of a subterranean cult. Beneath the villa excavators found a room in which niches in the walls had been painted with the elaborate figures of three naked water nymphs accompanied by a symbolic entourage of dolphins.

However, the Romans demonstrated practical, as well as ritual, uses for their water supplies in one of the most radical new habits to be introduced to Britain – bathing. Daily washing was an unfamiliar concept to native Britons, whose standards of personal hygiene must have appalled the fastidious continentals. The Romans, on the other hand, had turned bathing into a refined and time-consuming art. In a pattern repeated right across the empire, public bath-houses were constructed which, for a small fee, were open to all. Bath-houses were fundamental to the daily routines of everyone from military commanders to slaves. Inside, they were much like the modern sauna but this was more than just a place to get clean; people relaxed here after work, met friends and discussed politics or business.

A complex series of rooms of varying temperature and humidity were on offer as well as hot and cold plunge baths but the secret to Roman bath-houses lay in the hypocaust system. Hot air from a furnace was ingeniously circulated between columns supporting a tiled floor and up flues within hollow tiled walls. By moving to progressively hotter, steamier rooms, clients would develop a sweat. Their skin was then covered in oil which, along with sweat and accumulated dirt, was scraped off with a curved metal blade. All forms of ablution, even hair removal, were catered for and a masseur was always on hand to release the tensions of the day. But there are suggestions that activities of a less than purifying nature also took place within bath-houses.

In the cold room of the bath-house at Netherby in North Yorkshire, near a mural of a man whose toga appeared to have slipped, an altar was found dedicated to Fortuna, goddess of gambling. Dice, bone counters and coins found in the drains of bath-houses bear witness to a pastime so indulged-in that edicts had to be issued against it. Groans from weight lifters competed with the shouts of gamblers and the slapping of masseurs' hands on pummelled flesh. The Roman writer, Seneca, described the sounds issuing from a nearby bath house as 'enough to make one sick' and it is tempting to wonder what else went on inside the bath-houses but, intriguingly, he added, 'It would disgust me to give details.'

It is obvious, from the number of hairpins and articles of jewellery found washed into the drains along with the gambling pieces, that both sexes used the baths. Officially, men and women were supposed to visit at different times but it seems that occasionally things got a little out of hand. Written accounts testify that, perhaps not surprisingly in a place where people were getting naked and steamed up, the authorities sometimes had to be called in to restore decency and order.

But this new fashion also resulted in some of the most architecturally magnificent structures of the Roman Empire. The entire city of Bath owes its name to such a building, as it was here that the Romans constructed what was hailed as the grandest bathing establishment in western Europe. The Aquae Sulis elegantly combined a temple to Sulis – synonymously dedicated to the imperial goddess Minerva – with an enormous suite of bathing pools representing the zenith of Roman water management. From a thermal spring rising in the south-east corner of the temple precinct, over two million litres of hot water flowed every day to the public baths through a series of channels and lead pipes. The high vaulted ceiling has now collapsed so the main pool is roofed by the sky. On a cold autumn day the naturally heated water – which still flows at the same impressive rate – is shrouded with swirls of eddying steam. Although visitors are now strongly encouraged to remain fully clothed, it takes little imagination to hear the voices of bathers echoing between the columned walls as they took their first plunge into steaming hot water.

Ritual and religion were also important at bath-houses elsewhere in the country. At Chesters in Northumberland, from a terrace bustling with barrack blocks and administrative buildings, the ground slopes gently down to a wide bend in the North Tyne river. Here, near the foot of the slope, the finely dressed masonry blocks of the lower bath-house courses survive. In what was the changing room, seven elegant niches large enough to sit in are carved into the wall. These probably formed altars housing a selection of venerated statuettes – not an unexpected feature given what we know about the superstitious nature of the Roman people; a little more surprising, though, on the wall of an adjacent room, is a shockingly graphic depiction.

The surface of one stone in the lowest course of the bath-house wall has been neatly carved away leaving a small but unmistakable penis and testicles. This image of male genitalia, which seems to have been made beneath the level of the floor, would not have been visible once the tiles were in place above the hypocaust system. The sophistication of the architecture and the heating and plumbing supplies make it easy to forget that these are ancient remains but, barely five centimetres in length, this tiny human symbol carved in stones has survived for nearly two

Chiselled into stone at Housesteads Roman fort, this military-style phallus stands upright in a regimental display of virility.

thousand years. As an image the phallus is universally recognisable even by cultures separated by nineteen centuries of history, but why was it carved here? Was it added in humour by the builders of the bath-house, or was this a more meaningful emblem embedded in the fabric of the new building for a specific reason?

The phallic carving at Chesters bath-house, though, is not an isolated example. A few miles further west, on the crest of a high ridge of basaltic rock known as the Whin Sill, is the magnificent Roman fort of Housesteads. With expansive views over a wild, open landscape, the hilltop fort occupies an exhilaratingly

117

strategic position. Even in this exposed place someone felt compelled to add to the stones their enduring emblem of masculinity.

The interior of the fort is still covered with the stone foundations of regimental lines of military structures: barrack blocks, a grain store and the central headquarters building. The fort was accessed on each of the four sides via a guarded gateway and grooves worn in the flagstones testify to the number of heavily laden cartloads that must have rumbled over the thresholds. Excavators have determined that three blocks of living quarters in the north-east corner of the fort were, at some stage, converted into what looks like a barn. At the far end of the block, beside the east gate, a small bath-house was built and one of its wall stones was endowed with a very erect phallus. Chiselled into the rock, and described in 1831 as 'looking like a pair of spectacles', this military-style phallus stands completely upright in a regimental display of virility. It is improbable that the Chesters and Housesteads engravings were the work of the same artist, but is possible that there is a common meaning behind them?

The iconography of the Roman period differs from its prehistoric forerunners in one fundamental aspect. Britain, prior to invasion from the continent, was a country with no written culture. With the arrival of the Romans came the ability to record facts, ideas and fiction in a way other than through oral tradition. Two thousand years later, we know exactly what these images meant to the people who carved them.

Romans, as we know, were superstitious people. Unseen powers, the forces of good and evil, manifested themselves in an unfamiliar environment that was far from secure. A desire to influence these potentially malevolent forces, to overcome them and to encourage good fortune in their place resulted in the emergence of a phallic cult. To a patriarchal society, led by emperors and defended by soldiers, the most potent sign imaginable must have been the root of their masculinity, the source of their power and male lineage. The simple phalluses carved in stone were not pornographic or even erotic. They were symbols of strength against the forces of evil, totems of fertility and good luck.

The bath-house walls at Chesters and Housesteads may well have been adorned with erect penises to protect men in their vulnerable state, undressed and unarmed. But they also appeared on other public buildings and were carved into shop fronts; large phalluses were painted inside homes, and smaller ones were engraved into furniture. Archaeologists combing the fields of Lanarkshire found Samian pottery decorated with a man bearing an enormous erect penis, and in a fashion that would seem outrageous today, tiny phalluses cast in bronze and silver were

In Roman Britain, the phallus was a potent symbol of good fortune. Superstitious soldiers must have stepped over this carving at Chesters army headquarters building, ensuring its survival for two thousand years.

even worn as earrings, necklaces and brooches. In their bewildering array of shape and size, penises, it seems, were everywhere.

The headquarters building at Chesters was once a very grand structure. Dominating the interior of the fort, its ground plan is now marked by some pillar bases and an area of paving. At one time this walkway must have thronged with soldiers and military commanders and each one of them must have been aware of one particular stone slab. A magnificent

A phallus was carved on
the east bridge abutment
at Chollerford in
Northumberland.

This well-defined carving survives on the Roman bridge abutment at Chollerford in Northumberland.

carved penis with conjoined testicles was displayed here in well-defined relief. That it shows little sign of wear might indicate that people passing on the pavement stepped across the phallic design, perhaps with deliberate superstitious intent, like walking around a ladder. Bearing in mind the adoption that took place of local, pre-Roman beliefs, it is also interesting that this phallus lies within a circle and points towards the male power of the rising sun in the east.

Here at Chesters, the North Tyne river was breached by two successive bridges. The first, built in AD 122 while the foundations of Hadrian's Wall were still being laid, was designed to carry the northern frontier barricade across the waters of the North Tyne on a series of eight elegant piers. But the bridge was destroyed, probably by severe floods, and in the mid-second century was replaced by a magnificent three-piered construction. The bridge is now ruinous and the shady, tree-lined eastern riverbank is strewn with enormous blocks of carefully chiselled masonry. Carved into the stonework of the eastern abutment and now hoary with lichen, is a beautifully formed phallus. Although this bridge was constructed by highly skilled stone masons with the help of the indomitable labour force of the imperial army, its builders still felt the need to protect their structure with a touchingly human emblem, an entreaty to the gods of good fortune.

Further to the west, on a sheltered terrace and bordered by a steep ravine, are some of the best preserved Roman remains in northern Britain. One of the earliest army bases in the area, Vindolanda was built a mile or so to the south of the line that Hadrian's Wall would later take. One of the most fundamental improvements introduced as a result of the invasion can still be seen here: a clean water supply and efficient drainage. Finely laminated blue slate slabs form pavements under which waste water and sewage were channeled safely in a municipal scheme to rival any modern town. Perhaps it is

appropriate that here the forces of evil were warded away with a miniature emblem of fortune. Hidden now amidst the grass, this tiny carved phallus, less than ten centimetres in length, adorns the lowest course of stonework on a drain in the north of the fort. This good luck token has evidently protected the drainage system for the past two thousand years.

Much of the stone used in the construction of Vindolanda was quarried from a hillside visible from the fort. Soldiers must have sweated and cursed alongside locals drafted in to assist with the building project as together they levered out blocks of stone to be crafted by masons. On the raw face of the quarry one of the workers left behind an enormous but oddly misshapen phallus. Crudely pecked into the rock as a series of gouged dots this priapic member is unfeasibly pointed with an unfortunate bulge near the base, where it joins two unevenly sized testicles. Any acclaim for creating such an outsized symbol of good fortune would surely have been offset by the ridicule from the artist's fellow quarry-workers at such a comically misshapen image.

When Hadrian's Wall was built across Britain – from Bowness-on-Solway in the west to Wallsend in the east – its line followed the naturally defensive geological fault of the Whin Sill ridge. With the added protection of a massive bank and ditch, the wall provided a fortified baseline for troops on the

Now hidden in the grass, this tiny carved phallus adorns the lowest course of stone in one of Vindolanda's drains.

northernmost frontier of the vast Roman empire. Sent to posts in this remote and hostile territory it is not surprising that soldiers feared malevolent forces and actively sought protection from more benign powers through the use of magic and symbolism.

Birdoswald fort lies in the heart of northern England, on the border between Cumbria and

One of a pair of phalluses that can be found carved into the south-facing side of Hadrian's Wall.

Northumberland. The wall here extends eastward across the dips and slopes of the natural landscape, unbending, to the middle distance and to two phalluses carved on the south-facing, safer, side of the wall. Could this indicate a desire to attract good fortune rather than to repel the evil forces that lurked on the other side of the frontier; or even just a reluctance to venture beyond the edge of the frontier? And the symbols themselves are personal rather than imperial; the contrast of the exposed member portrayed in rough stone emphasises the vulnerability of humans in a hostile territory and inhospitable weather.

Hundreds of miles of Roman routes were marked by milestones, as at Middleton in Cumbria.

The Serpent Stone, encompassing the triple imagery of phallus, head and serpent, is the most potent Roman symbol stone yet recovered.

Another phallus was also excavated from the Birdoswald fort. Originally occupying a position above a window arch, this was typical of the location of many carved Roman phalluses. Evil spirits might enter through entrances, gateways and arches so these were frequently guarded by these potent symbols of good fortune, but was there an additional explanation for their presence here? Bearing in mind the Celtic association between passages and the female form, it is conceivable that these openings were seen as the architectural equivalent of vaginas – the obvious consort of which was provided in the form of the carved phallus.

The omnipresent phallus, it seems, also pervaded other aspects of Roman structure. Hundreds of miles of tracks and roads were constructed as the army pushed the boundaries of the Empire further north and west. These routes were marked with stone pillars and, like their prehistoric predecessors, many of these were outrageously phallic in appearance. At Middleton in Cumbria a milestone was erected on a crest of gently rising ground overlooking the verdant valley of the River Lune. Undoubtedly a very efficient marker, this stone must also be appreciated for its other, more anthropomorphic, properties.

Phallic symbols of good fortune were not, however, always portrayed as straightforward male genitalia. In some cases, additions such as wings or legs were made that imbued the images with increased power. But perhaps the most impressive example is a pillar known as the Serpent Stone. Found at the cemetery of the coastal fort of Maryport in Cumbria, this phallus-shaped column stands over one metre in height. One side is carved with a human head – a clear indication of Celtic influence – while the reverse depicts the unmistakable outline of a serpent. This triple imagery of phallus, head and serpent is possibly the most potent symbol stone yet recovered from a Romano-British site.

A second stone recovered from Maryport, inscribed with an incredibly straight phallus and a vertical oval slit, has been interpreted as a depiction of penis and vulva. A similar carving was found at Chesters, but in this case a very anatomically correct phallus was accompanied by a more complex slit and ring design. It may be possible to extend the same interpretation to this stone but if either of these carvings do, indeed, portray imminent penetration then a whole new dimension has been added to the repertoire of so called innocent good luck charms. Rather than simply being abstract totems for warding off evil, the phalluses from Chesters and Maryport have reclaimed their humanness and are infused with rampant sexuality.

Throughout history, periods of war or unrest that displace military troops from their usual surroundings have often brought about localised sexual revolutions. The arrival in Britain of armies of men who were paid in cash and who spent long periods of time unoccupied between campaigns must have had a profound impact on people's sexual behavior. Each Roman fort in Britain had its attendant civilian settlement, or vicus. Often little more than a shantytown this was where army followers set up their shops, drinking houses and other establishments. A good living was no doubt to be made providing the bored and salaried soldiers with goods – or services.

There is no mention, in the oral history of the Celts, of any establishments prior to the invasion along the lines of a brothel, but in Roman society, sex was a highly organised industry. Italian cities such as Pompeii provide ample evidence for the regulated activities of sex professionals. Large buildings were subdivided into smaller, private apartments where liaisons took place. There is even evidence of the payment scheme in use: upon selection of the service desired, payment was taken by a cashier who issued, in exchange, a brothel token depicting that particular activity. Tokens were then surrendered to the prostitutes who could see exactly what service had been paid for – and some services were, naturally, more expensive than others.

But it would be cynical to think that unions were always a business arrangement. Although Roman

If imminent penetration is depicted here then this phallus is more than a totem of good luck – it is infused with rampant sexuality.

soldiers were at first forbidden to enter into marriage, there is evidence to suggest that the army failed to prevent love blossoming among the cold, grey stones of the imperial forts. Perhaps the most touching of these artefacts comes from Vindolanda in Northumberland. A jet betrothal medallion, found in an alleyway outside the walls of the mansio, or inn, was engraved with the heads of a man and woman who appear to be kissing. The other side depicts two hands, clasped tightly, in what may be a sign of the marriage bond. A ring was also found not far away inscribed with the words 'animiea mea' meaning 'my love' or 'my

soul'. Tiny statuettes of the goddess Venus excavated from the area surrounding the fort may also have once been carried as portable emblems of love. We cannot know if these tokens were exchanged between sweethearts separated only by the walls of the fort or by much greater distances within the Roman empire.

Clearly the Romans, like the Greeks before them, had none of the reservations about nudity and sexuality that the modern west has inherited from the Judaeo-Christian tradition. Naked bodies and sexual imagery were a common element of everyday life, and surprisingly this was nowhere more true than in the family home. With the development of palatial country houses, or villas, in the Romano-British landscape, an entirely new concept was introduced. For the first time it was desirable that living surroundings were not only functional but also beautiful. Gardens were created purely for pleasure and large sums of money were invested in sumptuously decorating the interior and outer walls of houses.

In a fashion that began in the central empire, travelling artists with their copybooks of designs embellished the walls of villas belonging to wealthy British landowners wishing to emulate the lavish Roman lifestyle. Although few compositions could compare with the pornographic, orgiastic scenes depicted on the walls of houses in Pompeii, these patrons of the arts were in no way coy about commissioning works that might raise a few eyebrows with designers today. At Low Ham in Somerset the mythological story of an affair between Dido and Aeneas was depicted in graphic detail. The courtyard of a house belonging to a wealthy businessman in Leicester was decorated with a continuous erotic frieze of birds, animals and humans in what is coyly described as 'Pompeian manner'.

An elegant mosaic from Fishbourne Palace near Chichester shows Cupid riding on the back of a dolphin – depicting a potent combination of love and fertility. Gardens were planted here in complex geometric patterns with water as an important element of the design. Pools and fountains were supplied with running water in emulation of the springs and wells so revered in the natural landscape. Privacy could easily have been found in these gardens that were divided into small, hedged compartments and niches would have been created to house figurines such as the bronze statuette of Venus found at Verulamium in modern St Albans. And even here, amongst the shrubs and flowers the symbol of good fortune re-emerged. Statues of Priapus, the Greek god of fertility, whose grotesquely huge penus was legendary, were placed in gardens to act as scarecrows. Wind chimes, or 'tintinabula', of bronze cast in the shape of a phallus adorned with tinkling bells, also believed to ward off evil, were hung in the gardens and porticoes of Romanesque homes.

As well as new ideas on home design the Romans introduced a pantheon of new religions. The triad of Jupiter, Juno and Minerva was officially observed along with a vast spectrum of other gods and goddesses from Graeco-Roman and Egyptian sources. Mithraism was perhaps the most prominent eastern religion with its strong associations with – very familiar sounding – bulls and the sun. The Celts previously had no history of permanent dedication of an individual's sexuality to a deity or of ritual virginity or castration. This was another

An elegant mosaic at Fishbourne Roman palace depicts Cupid riding on a dolphin – a heady combination of love and fertility.

new concept introduced to Britain from the continent. One burial excavated from the site of Cataractonium, now Catterick in North Yorkshire, had archaeologists very puzzled. Originally thought to be that of a woman, upon closer examination the remains turned out to be those of a castrated male. The body was richly adorned with a jet necklace of six hundred beads, a jet bracelet, an armlet of shale and a bronze anklet. This, it seems, was the body of a gallus – a priest of the goddess Cybele. In an expression of devotion apparently not seen before in Britain, galli wore women's clothes and jewellery – and ritually castrated themselves. Perhaps the small round pebbles found in the mouth of the deceased were symbolic of what had been lost in life.

Not surprisingly, this religion did not catch on. Christianity, on the other hand, did. Having spread from the central empire, this new religion eventually reached the shores of Britain. Early Christian shrines have been identified at South Shields and a timber-framed church – one of the first in the country – was built at Richborough in Kent. After continuous uprisings by the Picts, Scots and Irish, and raids from Germanic Saxons, the Roman army eventually withdrew from this most northerly province in the early fifth century AD. Having transformed a turbulent land of warring tribes into a prosperous and civilised province, they returned to the continental heart of the empire. But the Romans left behind the seeds of Christianity, appropriately, at the same place where troops had disembarked almost four hundred years earlier. And Christianity would dictate the development of sexual symbolism in the British landscape for the next sixteen hundred years.

At Kilsarken church in County Kerry, not only are there shrines to the Virgin Mary but also one to the church's female exhibitionist carving.

CHAPTER SIX

The Serpent in the Garden of Eden

CHRISTIANITY HAS DONE MUCH FOR LOVE BY MAKING IT A SIN.

ANATOLE FRANCE

Though water no longer flowed along regimented drainage channels in abandoned forts, it had never ceased to flow from natural springs and rivers of the Celtic landscape goddess. Beyond the imperial frontiers, now deserted, lay lands untouched by nearly four hundred years of Roman occupation. Despite the arrival of new engineering methods and even new deities, an undercurrent of Celtic culture had been kept alive in the remoter parts of Britain and Ireland. This folklore attested to a deep connection that, in many areas, still existed between the sexuality of the people and the fertile land.

In County Meath in the south-west of Ireland, a pair of hills, known as Da Cich na Morigna – or the Breasts of the Great Queen – still cast their fulsome shadow over a people who venerated the female land. Named after Morrigan, a mythological fury and goddess of war and lust, the powerful presence of the hills is a reminder of legends in which the Celtic rules of sexual etiquette were transgressed.

Morrigan, together with Badbh and Macha, formed a trinity of war goddesses who would manifest themselves as crows. According to mythology, a heroic warrior named CúChulain rejected the lustful advances of the goddess Morrigan. Mortally wounded in battle soon afterwards, CúChulain bound himself to a stone pillar – a symbol of his phallus and source of his strength. So supported, he fought on until overcome by death but his enemies only dared approach the slain warrior

The arcs and swirls carved on the surface of the Turoe Stone have been interpreted as abstract depictions of semen.

after Morrigan, in the form of a skald crow, landed on his body and pecked at his flesh, thereby claiming her revenge. This incident is only one from the mass of legends surrounding Celtic deities and mortal heroes, but it serves to illustrate that the land was perceived as a sexual form and, indeed, that phallic stones persisted into the post-Roman period as a symbol of fertility and strength.

Near the town of Loughrea in Galway stands a pillar that is probably unique amongst the ancient stones of Britain and Ireland. The Turoe Stone is a stout, bulbous column barely one metre tall, though its generic erectness is perhaps sufficient to consider it a legitimate component of Ireland's considerable phallic history. But it is not the shape of the pillar that has most excited scholars.

A triple incised line – or Greek key pattern – defines the fold of a foreskin above which the rounded head of the stone is carved with beautiful arcs and swirls. In a rapidly diminishing state of preservation, these flowing designs belong to a distinctive artistic style known as La Tène and are believed by some historians to be an abstract depiction of semen. The exact age of the carved stone is unknown. It may even date from the first century BC but what is significant about the Turoe Stone is that this elaborately decorated phallus was still revered centuries later when it was given pride of

Lia Fáil, the 'stone penis', was inextricably linked to the virility and power of Ireland's High Kings.

place within a ceremonial earthwork known as the Rath of Feerwore – or Enclosure of Great Men.

Not far from here, the role in Celtic society of similar ritual columns was so graphic as to be recorded not only in folklore but also in early written accounts. The Hill of Tara, or Temair, in County Meath, was the sacred dwelling place of the gods and seat of power of the High Kings of Ireland. Today, these lush, green slopes are covered in the visible remains of vast earthwork monuments dating back four and a half thousand years. Five roads once converged here and the gentle pastures, now grazed by sheep and cattle, still bear the marks of ancient enclosures or raths.

The most impressive of these is Rath Riogh – the Enclosure of the Kings.

Known as the Womb of Mother Ireland, the formidable earthwork encircles two smaller round enclosures and at its heart stands a pillar known as Lia Fáil – the Stone of Destiny. This phallic column was originally erected beside a prehistoric barrow, named the Mound of the Hostages, where its virile form brought symbolic life force to the metaphorically swollen belly of the mound. It was here, during the early centuries of the first millennium AD, that Ireland's High Kings were inaugurated in a ceremony that drew on the realms of mythology and left little to the imagination.

At that time, the fertility of the earth that supported these people was perceived as being inextricably linked to the virility of the king. Before being accepted, prospective leaders underwent a series of trials, one of which involved Lia Fáil. An eighth-century text, *De Shíl Chonairi Moir – Of the Race of Conaire Mór* – recounts a test that is reminiscent of King Arthur's legendary sword in the stone:

And Fal was there, the 'stone penis' at the head of the chariot-course; when a man should have the kingship of Tara, it screeched against his chariot-axle, so that all might hear . . . he who was not to hold Tara's kingship, the Fal would not screech against his axle.

In Irish mythology, the goddess Medb symbolised the sovereignty of Tara in female manifestation. She represented the union between the rightful king of Tara and his land, and the investiture of each new king demanded his successful ritual mating. The goddess's name was also associated with intoxication. By offering new leaders a drink then mating with them, she legitimised the reign of the king. Early Christian chroniclers describe a group of women at Tara whom they mistakenly referred to as 'nuns'. These, in fact, were priestesses of the goddess Medb who also served the needs of the High Kings. Until the adoption of Christianity in the sixth century, inauguration ceremonies seem to have actually brought the mythological fertility rites to life when a priestess, chosen to represent the goddess Medb, publicly copulated with the new king.

Long after the ceremonies at Tara had acquired a less adult theme, stone pillars continued to inspire a deeply rooted veneration of their phallic properties. The village of Newton is a rural community in Aberdeenshire with the air of a place that has elegantly evaded the passing of time. The whine of traffic along a distant modern road does not pervade

Letters from an ancient alphabet are inscribed upon the Newton Ogham Stone.

the tranquillity of a shady garden clearing in which two magnificent columns evoke all the potency of much earlier prehistoric standing stones.

Enclosed by statuesque trees and an impenetrable evergreen hedge, these two pillars stand like actors frozen, motionless, on a leafy stage. Their smooth surfaces have an almost iridescent quality in the light of late afternoon as yellow lichen blends with undertones of blue-grey gneiss. One column, known as the Newton Ogham Stone, is inscribed with six horizontal lines of mysterious characters. Letters of the ancient ogham alphabet are also inscribed vertically down its length. Devised in Ireland in the fourth century, the ogham script consisted of a series of lines and notches incised along a single line. Four hundred years later this alphabet was adopted by the Picts and inscribed upon the Newton Stone.

Beside it stands an intricately carved Pictish symbol stone dating to around the seventh century AD. The sculptural art of the Picts – from Shetland in the north to Fife in the south and as far west as the Hebridean Islands – was outstanding for its richness and originality. Their geometric symbols and highly stylised depictions of animals and birds with curling limbs and glaring eyes were skilfully carved on surfaces of natural, undressed stone. But these patterns were not the product of artistic fancy. The occurrence of the stylistically similar images

The Newton Pictish symbol stone is strikingly phallic and bears the serpent – an ancient symbol of sexuality.

throughout the Pictish region indicates that symbol stones held a deep significance whose meaning was widely agreed and understood. Part of that expression was clearly embodied in the particular stones chosen to be carved.

The stones at Newton, with their eerie and mysterious marks, are both strikingly phallic in appearance and from certain angles the reasoning behind their selection is unmistakable.

Although Celtic traditions were to continue throughout the Middle Ages in many parts of Britain and Ireland, the years following the departure of the Romans also brought profound change. In the subsequent political vacuum, struggles erupted among local leaders eager for control. While the north came under increasing pressure from Pictish tribes, the western seaboard was under attack from Ireland and tribes from Saxon Germany and the Angle territory of Schleswig-Holstein invaded the south. Farming communities faced dangers and turmoil which established beliefs could not explain. In these troubled times, another import from the continent was also gathering strength. It presented people with an alternative paradigm, and many now turned for guidance in their lives to a new religion – Christianity.

Many druids – the spiritual leaders of Celtic society – found that early Christian ideas were not necessarily at odds with their own. Christ could be identified with epic heroes such as CúChulain, the Old Testament was not dissimilar to the epic sagas of oral tradition, and baptism reflected the sacred associations held by water. By no means all the new doctrine was adopted by minds more accustomed to animistic concepts. People still looked to native customs to supplement the scriptures but Celtic traditions gradually merged with early Christianity into a hybrid religion, known as Celtic Christianity, that proved attractive to the masses. These mixed origins can be clearly seen in the many early stone crosses found throughout Great Britain and Ireland that, while obviously Christian in intent, are surprisingly carnal in their appearance.

At Penhale Sands near Perranporth in Cornwall, Saint Piran's Cross stands amidst a shifting ocean of dunes overlooking the Irish Sea. This textured shaft of stone was erected in the fifth century at the reputed landing place of Saint Piran. The buried city of Langarrow is also said to lie beneath these sands, buried along with its people in a storm over one thousand years ago as punishment for the wickedness of the inhabitants. Today, the erect and finely crafted column with its bulbous top seems curiously familiar – reminiscent, perhaps, of older, pagan stones. And St Piran's Cross is not an isolated example.

In the apparent emptiness of the Devonshire moors stands the striking outline of Bennett's Cross. The

St Piran's Cross near Perranporth is an early Christian stone with very obvious pagan origins.

139

Long Tom is known as one of the most explicit pillars in the British Isles. Its form bridges the evolutionary gap between pagan standing stones and the Celtic Christian cross.

intrinsically phallic appearance of this gnarled and sinuous pillar has barely been reduced by its formation into the recognisable emblem of a cross. But perhaps de-sexualisation of the stone was not the intention here. Early Christianity was, after all, heavily influenced by Celtic customs and a strong element of continuity blurred the boundary between them. People would be more open to adopting new practices if these were associated with familiar objects and places. So, early Christian stones may have been deliberately designed to emulate the stone phallus – that ancient symbol of divine fertility and strength. The landscape of Britain and Ireland is actually littered with phallic Christian pillars but it was not only in stone crosses that the iconography of the phallus lingered.

Caldey Island lies in Carmarthen Bay just off the Pembrokeshire coast in Wales. A monastery was founded here in the sixth century AD and, fifteen hundred years later, monks in white robes still live and work here in a modern monastic complex. The Priory Church of Saint Illtud was built here in the thirteenth century and still stands today. Its neatly coursed stones rise in a tower that is topped by an unmistakably phallic spire – an eloquent testimony to the lasting influence of Celtic symbolism.

In AD 597, Saint Augustine was sent to Britain. After landing in Kent, his tour allegedly brought Augustine to a small village in the county of Dorset.

The top of Bennett's Cross in Devonshire barely detracts from the graphic nature of this stone.

Here, in the shadow of a hill that possibly already bore the enormous and virile outline of the Cerne Abbas Giant, he struck the ground with his staff. Water, it was said, miraculously gushed from the earth, and what became known as St Augustine's Well grew into a site of Christian pilgrimage.

It was no accident that Augustine came to this spot. He was dispatched by Pope Gregory the Great with instructions to take over pagan temples and shrines as a means of encouraging people to attend their familiar places of worship – but as Christians. The waters that issued from the ground at Cerne Abbas came from a

141

Caldey Island's Priory Church of St Illtud has a spire that is clearly reminiscent of earlier standing stones.

natural spring that had, no doubt, been venerated by local people as the sacred life force of Mother Earth for countless generations.

And indeed, for centuries after Augustine the waters continued to be associated with natural powers. Drinking them was said to cure infertility and aid conception (a theory which the high natural iron content of the water may support). In a custom that has not only overtones of pagan sun worship but also of Christian baptism, it was believed to be beneficial to bathe a newborn baby in the pool at the moment its surface was touched by the first rays of morning sun. Young girls would go to the well to pray to Saint Catherine for a husband, turning round three times and, perhaps, running their fingers across the Catherine Wheel carved into the stones around the spring.

Attempts were made by the Christian church to sever ties to pagan sites. In the seventh century, the instructions of Theodore, Archbishop of Canterbury, were recorded in his *Penitentials* that 'no one shall go to trees, or wells, or stones, or enclosures, or anywhere else except to God's church, and there to make vows'. But the bond between native people and their landscape goddess was enduring.

In the eighth century a Northumbrian monk named Saint Baldred dwelt for some time on the Bass Rock, a huge geological formation that rises above the waves

Drinking the water from St Augustine's Well was said to cure infertility; young girls would come here to wish for a husband.

where the Firth of Forth meets the North Sea. When Saint Baldred was not on his rock he accepted thousands of pilgrims to his parish of Whitekirk in East Lothian. Although there is now little sign of a water source, many of these were women who claimed afterwards to have been cured of barrenness as a result of drinking from the spring there. At Madron in Cornwall, a holy well, which was reputed to have healing powers, was also visited in May by young girls hoping for a husband. Pairs of small, heavy objects, such as pins, were dropped into the water and if they stayed together as they sank, it was said, the girl and her sweetheart were also destined to stay together.

The adoption of new beliefs was by no means seamless. Christianity brought fundamental shifts in Celtic society in particular to attitudes towards sexuality. For centuries, Celtic attitudes towards sex had been open and relaxed. Copulation was celebrated as a natural part of life, intimately linked to the fecundity of the landscape and thereby all that was supported within it. In sharp contrast, Christian teachings isolated the sex drive both of men and women, associating it instead with immorality. Sex was no longer seen as a natural or loving act but as an undesirable urge that had to be controlled and, ultimately, conquered. The effects of this were profound, especially with regard to the social status of women. Sexually active females, previously venerated

as divine and voluptuous sources of fertility whose outlines were worshipped in the curves of hills and valleys, were relegated to the role of corrupting temptress.

By the tenth century, the pagan origins of many standing stones had been obliterated by the addition of Christian signs. On Caldey Island, Pembrokeshire, a deeply chiselled cross was added to a sixth-century ogham stone, and a round-topped stone pillar that stands near the church of Gleann Cholm Cille, in County Donegal in Ireland, was artistically sanctified by the addition of a more elaborately carved design. Ironically, in its tirade against fornication, the medieval church created a wealth of overtly sexual material, the legacy of which can still be found today.

At Maen Achwyfan in Clwyd, North Wales, is a stone cross dating to the tenth or possibly eleventh century. Although now greatly eroded, an image can be discerned in relief that, at face value, looks surprisingly irreligious. Carved into a panel at the base is what scholars of medieval iconography describe as a mega-phallic male exhibitionist. The phrase barely needs explanation though its theme is underlined by the symbolic presence of entwining serpents. If the appearance of such a figure is unexpected on a religious object like the Maen Achwyfan cross, then even more surprising is the decoration of medieval churches with similar carvings.

In what probably started as a continental fashion in France and Spain, many Romanesque churches in western Europe were richly adorned with carvings of figures very obviously displaying their genitals. These astonishingly immodest figures, both male and female in form, are grotesquely ugly in appearance, with exaggerated heads and genitals. Collectively termed 'exhibitionist' carvings they are perhaps better known as sheela-na-gigs.

One of the most famous sheela-na-gigs can be seen on the parish church at Kilpeck in Herefordshire. Standing in what was once the Welsh kingdom of Ergyng, this tranquil church is formed of a deep red sandstone that radiates the evening sun. Its architecture is pleasingly simple, with a stepped construction and semicircular apse. The exact foundation date is unknown but the present church is at least 850 years old and incorporates parts of an earlier, pre-Norman, structure within its fabric. On the south wall of the apse is an exquisitely carved gnomish character with a large, triangular head and bulging eyes. Her arms loop behind the knees of diminutive legs so that her fingers part the labia of an outrageously oversized vulva. She is known locally as 'the whore', and as this may not seem like a particularly suitable subject to be adorning the walls of a church, how did she end up in this unlikely position?

Kilpeck Church, over 850 years old, is adorned with immodest characters such as this one known locally as 'the whore'.

145

Kilpeck Church: exhibitionist carvings are thought to be a warning to parishioners against immoral behaviour.

Numerous explanations for exhibitionist figures have been put forward in recent years. The stylised appearance of examples such as the Kilpeck exhibitionist has led to the suggestion that they may be the vestigial idols of a pre-Christian religion. As the mother goddess was anciently depicted by the cardinal elements of belly and breasts, it has been proposed that these vulvae may have been the powerful symbol of an early fertility cult. Although the styling of these carvings may display similarities with Celtic art their content indicates otherwise.

It has also been suggested that these are good luck symbols, protective talismans or even the work of mischievous stone masons. But the most widely accepted explanation is, ironically, one of morality. The universal Catholic church taught that after death came judgement and then, depending on how the deceased had lived their short span on earth, there followed either heaven or hell. Mortals needed to conduct themselves in a way that – according to the church – ensured everlasting bliss, and these carvings may have been a warning against sins that could result in the alternative of eternal torture.

Exhibitionist carvings form only part of the rich language of visual imagery employed by a moralising church during the Middle Ages. Columns flanking the elaborate south door of Kilpeck church are clearly carved with snakes, the tail of one in the mouth of the other. The Celts, who believed in the spirits of nature and the importance of fertility and new life at springtime, venerated serpents, who sloughed their skin each year, as symbolising the continuing cycles of life. They also appear, entwined, around the intricately carved west window, but had perhaps been Christianised into a symbol of new life through redemption. There are also some blank spaces where clearly carvings have been removed. The local story behind these gaps is that a Victorian lady was so offended by them – presumably the figures were naked or exhibitionists – that she had them knocked them off the walls of the church.

A later connection with fertility customs may be supported by an appealing figure on All Saints' Church at Buckland in Buckinghamshire. This peaceful village lies on the edge of the Chiltern hills by the route of the Icknield Way, one of the oldest track ways in the country. The parish church dates to the late thirteenth century but in the 1800s the Reverend Edward Bonus decided that it would be improved by the addition of gothic-style gargoyles. These 'Victorian monstrosities' glare from the corners of the tower so arrestingly that anyone approaching the church could be forgiven for not noticing a much smaller figure set in the wall below. A piece of stone, carved with an endearing but badly worn exhibitionist, nestles among flint nodules above

An exhibitionist carving nestles among flint nodules above the Priests' Door of All Saints' Church in Buckland.

147

The endearing Buckland exhibitionist is badly eroded but the gaping vaginal opening is still unmistakable.

the Priest's Door in the south wall. Grinning as she pulls open a gaping vulvular hole, this crude little carving appears to have been eroded not by weathering but by the rubbing of many hands over her pudenda. Given her lofty position, requiring a small ladder to be reached, these were not idle, passing strokes but deliberate actions, probably in the hope of invoking fertility or safe childbirth.

Another medieval character whose genitals have evidently been the subject of much tactile attention can be found on a church in Kilsarken in County Kerry. Hidden amongst the verdant fields and narrow, winding lanes of this remote corner of Ireland is a ruined, roofless church. Stones that must once have resounded with the sound of hymn singing are now colonised by orange and grey lichens and wetted with rain. Above one window is a carefully engraved figure with a surprised expression and pointed ears. The spreading arch represents her legs so that the entire window forms the opening to her womb. The tip of the archway and its vertical sides have been heavily rubbed in a manner reminiscent of the Buckland figure. Nearby shrines to the Virgin Mary are strewn with flowers but there is also a shrine to the Kilsarken exhibitionist. It seems curious that, in a country steeped in Catholicism, an ancient and immodest symbol is revered alongside the Blessed Virgin.

These female exhibitionists may seem

Although Kilsarken Church in County Kerry is now ruinous, a female exhibitionist carving or sheela-na-gig, survives above the narrow central window in its south wall.

The entire window arch forms the vaginal opening between the legs of the Kilsarken sheela-na-gig.

inappropriate decoration for church walls but some of the male examples are equally explicit. At Abson in South Gloucestershire, among the regular courses of neatly dressed stone on the south wall of the church, is a rather unnerving figure. Crawling on all fours is a man whose erection protrudes from between his legs. His unhappy face is turned to fix the observer with a penetrating stare; the resulting effect is definitely more pathos than Eros.

A similar carving, on Whittlesford Church near Cambridge, underlines a suspicion that these images were never intended as erotic or to arouse feelings of sexual passion. Many people over the past eight hundred years must have glanced up at the engraved lintel that spans a round-arched Norman window below the tower clock. The scene depicted here may seem more shocking to us today than to medieval churchgoers when the meaning behind it would have been understood. A fat, bald woman squats with her legs splayed to reveal a vulvular slit. Her right hand passes under her buttock and her fingers are inserted into the opening. A bearded ithyphallic male crawls towards her in reaction to her invitation and mating, we can see, is imminent. But his elongated shape and crouched approach create a repellent and bestial scene designed to quell all thoughts of romance in the minds of medieval parishioners. Perhaps this depiction echoes the belief among many Christian

Whittlesford Church is carved with both male and female figures whose intentions towards one another are quite clear.

medieval chroniclers that women's sensuality was the gateway to eternal damnation.

Exhibitionist carvings, it seems, were actually warnings against the sins they portrayed; an unpleasant image of the vice was intended to encourage the opposed virtue. Far from being immoral these depictions are, in fact, extremely moralistic; one was even carved on the outer wall of the nunnery on Iona. Medieval people, although largely illiterate, were accustomed to finding meanings hidden in visual symbols, and these were often warnings against the deadly sins of the flesh or 'luxuria'. Monkeys carved on roof bosses and corbels were symbolic of bestiality and lust and flaming torches signified lechery. A struggle between vice and virtue was often depicted as a conflict between men and beasts in a language of symbolism that found widespread expression in the religious establishment of the British Isles.

Carved in stone at the base of Prior Leschman's Chantry in Hexham Abbey in Northumberland is a grotesque three-faced man. With a codpiece between his legs he sits astride a demonic beast with lolling tongue and cloven feet. His three faces seem to represent a warning against the depravities of lust: the temptations of youth, disillusionment of middle age and despair of death. Even mermaids, such as the one carved on a bench end in Zennor in Cornwall, were

not what they seemed. In his twelfth-century work, *Bestiary*, Pierre le Picard wrote of the sailors lured to their doom by the beauty and song of enchanting sirens. Mermaids represented the dangers faced by men in being drawn to disaster by seductive women.

It is surprising that the Whittlesford carving, described as 'so gross a spectacle . . . it would look indecent even in a bordello', and others like it, are still in place today. Britain and Ireland were at one time covered in similar imagery but such carvings were targets of puritanical attacks by Victorian iconoclasts outraged by what they saw as obscene material. Often only those in high and inaccessible places survived. The same symbolism, though, was evidently taken beyond the bounds of the local churchyard and into the vernacular world outside.

Anyone walking along Palace Street in Canterbury may be surprised if they stop outside number 8 and raised their eyes above street level: their inquisitive gaze will be met by a bare-breasted female. This bawdy exhibitionist figurine is carved into a wooden corbel beneath the overhanging second floor but she is no vision of loveliness. Although hands clasp her breasts, pushing them forward in an unmistakably provocative manner, a longer look will reveal a strangely masculine character with grotesquely swollen lips, pointed, satyr-like ears and cloven hooves. This devilish figure was not designed to tempt. It seems, instead, to have been the work of a wood carver intent on turning people from being tempted by the sins of the flesh.

By the late thirteenth century the church had grown less tolerant of enduring pagan practices. Despite the adoption of sexual imagery which today may seem confusing, the church remained resolute that its flock would be discouraged from having any association with sites linked to the ancient worship of sexuality. As part of this process, prehistoric stones, which for generations had been inextricably bound to natural rites of fertility, were given new names that associated them with unsuitable company.

At the great stone circle of Avebury, one huge monolith formerly referred to as the Wishing Stone was labelled the Devil's Chair. The northern cove became known as the Devil's Brand-irons and the Beckhampton Cove was dubbed the Devil's Coits. Not satisfied with demonising the stones in the minds of superstitious people, the church then encouraged villagers to destroy these ancient monuments. But a cautious respect for the old religion clearly deterred people from smashing the stones and instead they were toppled and buried out of sight.

One unfortunate itinerant barber-surgeon, travelling the countryside with the tools of his trade, joined in the misguided work at Avebury and was crushed by one of the stones as it fell to the ground.

A wooden figure carved under the first-floor eaves of Palace Street in Canterbury is both sexual and grotesque.

His neck and pelvis were broken and no attempt was made to recover the body from where he lay with his scissors, probe and silver pennies dated 1307 AD. When Christian zealots had finished exorcising the pagan past from the Avebury circle this formerly sacred place became the site of a market. In a parody of the well-known biblical story in which Christ turned moneylenders out of the temple, one of the fallen megaliths was used as a cold slab for selling fish.

The church was mistaken, though, if it thought that by Christianising pagan stones and discouraging people from attending pagan sites, the old links between sex and the landscape would be discarded in exchange for a sermon on the sins of the flesh. Instead, some ancient customs were taken into the very heart of the community. Throughout the Middle Ages, trees were venerated as embodying the spirit of fertility, perhaps because their sturdy, erect trunks mirrored the properties of the phallus, or because their leaves, regenerating each year at spring, encapsulated the essence of renewal. The climax of spring festivals was May Day, held usually, but not always, on the first day of the month, when the fertility of the awakening earth was reaffirmed in celebrations.

By the sixteenth century, deep rifts had formed within the church between those who followed the Catholic doctrine and those who demanded reform. Eventually, England severed connections with Rome and the Anglican church was formed. Like the establishment that preceded it, however, this church found the continuation of pagan customs increasingly unacceptable.

According to accounts of the period, in the early hours before dawn on May Day young men and women would venture into the woods 'to practise the emotive and symbolic ritual of orgiastic mating similar to that which took place in the fields at sowing time'. One disgusted Puritan complained, in 1583, that 'all the yung men and maides, olde men and wives, run gadding about over night to the woods, groves, hils, and mountains where they spend all the night in plesant pastimes'. He added 'that of fortie, threescore, or a hundred maides going to the wood over night, there have scaresly the third part of them returned home againe undefiled'. Trees would also be cut down by the enthusiastic hordes, who returned to the village with spring blossoms, greenery and this 'may pole', which our puritan described as a 'stinking ydol'.

The dancing and feasting that followed were only part of a festival intended to concentrate the physical energies of mass copulation in the countryside into one symbolic act of procreation. The forces of nature, it was hoped, would be encouraged to respond in empathetic fruitfulness. The civilised dancing with plaited ribbons still practised in some villages today

The erection of maypoles was banned by Puritans in 1664 but Ickwell in Bedfordshire is one of the many villages in Britain where May Day celebrations still take place.

was a Victorian attempt to add a veneer of innocence to events, and must bear little resemblance to the open-air orgies of previous centuries. Unlike many other pagan ceremonies that were adopted by the church, the May Day festivals were too blatantly sexual to ever be incorporated into a Christian calendar. Although by 1644 the Puritans had succeeded in banning celebrations involving maypoles, in some villages such as Ickwell in Bedfordshire and Bledington in Gloucestershire, this phallic emblem of the living tree can still be seen today.

In one hand the Ballycloghduff figure brandishes a key and in the other he clasps an over-sized phallus.

In rural communities the phallus also reared its head in a slightly different form. Gateposts throughout Northern Ireland were traditionally suggestively shaped. Entrances to fields, farmyards and even lanes are still flanked by pillars clearly endowed with rounded or conical heads and the logic behind these seems to have been to ensure the fertility of beasts driven between them. An unusual gatepost at Ballycloghduff in central Ireland incorporates a male exhibitionist figure, carved in stone. In one hand he brandishes a key while in the other he clasps his enormously over-sized penis. The origins of this figure are a mystery and even his meaning remains obscure. Did he intimate to a medieval audience that the key to eternal heaven lies in earthly sexual restraint or was he offering his blatant sexuality to the livestock being herded past?

The enduring connection between certain stones and human sexuality was recorded orally in folklore and expressed in customs that surrounded the major rites of passage of marriage and childbirth. In many rural areas these customs were upheld as recently as the beginning of the twentieth century.

One of the enormous monoliths at the southern entrance to the Avebury circle was known as the Wishing Stone. In a ritual that echoes the spring mating of Avebury's original users, on the eve of May Day, adolescent girls would come here to sit in a large hollow in the stone in the hope of securing themselves a husband. This superstitious act was evidently not deterred by the church's efforts to link it with the devil and was carried out by young girls at Avebury until the 1930s.

Holed stones seem to have held particularly strong links when it comes to matters of mating. Their patently coital appearance, coupled with the height at which the holes often occur, has led to the suggestion that these stones were originally used for ceremonies involving the ritual insertion of a penis. In later centuries, the perforation was given a less graphic but nonetheless symbolic role. At Doagh in the Irish county of Antrim stands a tapering stone whose sandy-coloured surface is deeply scored with lines, as though wrinkled with age. Marriages were traditionally sanctioned here by the clasping of hands through a hole in the middle of the stone. Betrothals were also made at the Plightin Stane, at Lairg in Sutherland, which – perhaps in an attempt to Christianise the stone – was actually built into the wall of the church.

In rural communities, where fertility and reproduction were of paramount importance, marriages were only considered successful if their consummation resulted in pregnancy and women went to extraordinary lengths to ensure that it did. Warton Hill in Lancashire is a magnificent natural outcrop of limestone. Taking a seat in a particular natural hollow at the foot of the limestone rocks, it was believed, would ensure that the woman bore children.

Assurance that marriages would be fruitful was similarly sought on Holy Island off the coast of Northumberland. The Petting Stone is the moss-covered base of an old market cross which stands next to the church. In a wedding tradition that still continues today, couples were expected to leap over the stone but it was taken as a bad omen if the bride was unable to clear the stone. The King Stone at the Rollright circle in Oxfordshire also acquired sexual powers. Here, childless wives would rub their bare breasts against the cold, rough stone in a ritual believed to aid conception.

Perhaps because they were anciently associated with another right of passage – that from this world to the afterlife – women would also look to the many sacred stones of Britain and Ireland to ensure a trouble-free childbirth. In the Scottish Highlands north of Braemar lie the Cairngorm Mountains. Here, on the northern side of a granite peak named Ben Avon, is a rocky tor called Clach Bahn where millions of years of erosion have weathered the rock into an incredible formation of natural seats and pools. Women living in distant valleys would travel here to climb the rugged, blustery heights of Clach Bahn and

Failure to leap over the Holy Island Petting Stone was believed to be the omen of an unfruitful marriage.

sit in the sculpted stony seats in the hope of easing the imminent pain of childbirth.

It may be coincidence that many of these places are measurably rich in negative ions – particles believed to have a physical benefit both to health in general and to fertility in particular. Whether or not a sense of this was behind the development of such traditions, a superstitious link between sex and the landscape continued to be observed in fields, hills and woodlands many centuries after the Synod of Whitby in AD 663 forbade the practice of Celtic customs. But Britain was a heavily stratified society and while the church endeavoured to save its rural flock from pagan sins of the flesh, an entirely different concept was developing amongst the upper echelons – that of 'noble love'.

By the late Middle Ages, the church's strong disapproval of people getting acquainted in the Biblical sense ultimately led to carnal relationships falling out of fashion. Outwardly, sexual behaviour – at least in public – was no longer acceptable in high society and the healthy Celtic romp was replaced with the romantic ideal of noble, or courtly love. Emphasis shifted from consummation to the expression of chivalrous values such as virtue and honour. These became embodied, through the fifteenth-century writings of Sir Thomas Malory, in the mist-shrouded figure of King Arthur.

Arthur is probably the most famous of all the inhabitants of medieval Britain. Based upon a fifth-century leader who defended Britain against Anglo-Saxon invasion, he was the central character of Malory's *Le Morte d'Arthur*. Since then, stories of his noble deeds have become inextricably woven into myth and history alike, making it difficult sometimes to separate fact from fantasy. His love for Guinevere, so celebrated in later medieval romance, was a tragic one ending in one of literature's most infamous acts of adultery. The western British Isles resound with stories of King Arthur but perhaps nowhere is more strongly associated with the myths than Tintagel Castle.

On Cornwall's jagged north coast, the castle of Tintagel is perched perilously on the edge of cliffs that plunge down to echoing coves where black, spray-drenched rocks lurk in brilliant turquoise water. An alarmingly steep flight of rock-hewn steps winds down the cliff face to ascend once more, through a heavy wooden door in a curtain wall, on to the summit of a defended craggy stack. The ocean crashes on every side and, in the summer months, a dense sea mist can appear seemingly from nowhere, obscuring the mainland. Cut off and shrouded at such times in a sound-muting time capsule of impenetrable air, this rocky citadel provides a fitting backdrop to the legend of Arthur and Guinevere.

This, however, is not the only tale of tragic love to survive among romantic ruins. Lying within a bend of the River Coquet in Northumberland is the forbidding fortification of Warkworth Castle. But this indomitable façade softens in the evening sun when its sandstone radiates a warm yellow glow and a closer look reveals a very human story.

A tightly winding pathway descends behind the castle to follow the course of the river. To one side are the green, deep and slow-moving waters while on the other lie fields that were once the deer park and hunting grounds of the Earl of Northumberland. Less than half a mile from the castle, the river bank on the far side rises to a natural vertical sandstone cliff and there, sculpted into its undulating face, is a doorway. A bower of sombre yew trees shades a flight of moss-covered steps that lead up to the doorway, above which a fourteenth-century Latin inscription, now eroded beyond comprehension, is said to have read 'Tears have been my meat day and night'. Through the low doorway is a series of gothic chambers beautifully hewn out of solid bedrock and dominated by what appears to be an altar – this is the Warkworth Hermitage, and its origins are as intiguing as its approach.

In his famous ballad of 1771, *The Hermit of Warkworth*, Bishop Percy tells of a noble Northumbrian warrior, Bertram, who, four hundred years earlier, had been enamoured of the fair Isabel of

Tintagel Castle on Cornwall's jagged north coast has become interwoven with legends of King Arthur's love for Guinevere and one of literature's most infamous acts of adultery.

Widdrington. But their love was ill-fated and the epic story ended in Bertram mistakenly slaying his beloved brother and his sweetheart. In grief and penitence Bertram created the Chapel, Confessional, and Dormitory as a mausoleum to Isabel where he lived the rest of his life in solitary devotion and mournful prayer. Bishop Percy described the memorial:

> Beside the altar rose a tomb
> All in the living stone;
> On which a young and beauteous maid
> In goodly sculpture shone . . .

A timeworn recumbent effigy can still be seen in the sill of a rock-cut window. It is said that a bull's head at her feet represents the crest of the Widdrington family and beneath that, on his knees with head bowed and one hand on his breast, is the grieving warrior himself.

As with King Arthur and Tintagel, it is not clear to what extent the origins of the Hermitage have been embroidered for purely literary effect. The atmosphere on this shady part of the river bank is certainly conducive to melancholy and records show that a resident hermit named George Lancastre was still using the chambers for devotional prayer in the 1530s.

Throughout history, seemingly unconnected events have combined, on occasion, with surprising consequences. So it was that around 1150, a warm climatic epoch coincided with a period of economic affluence and stability and the result was the development of the medieval pleasure garden.

The personal taste of the monarch had always influenced contemporary fashion and it was imperative that rulers on this side of the English Channel were seen to be in step with fashions on the continent. Kings from Henry II to Edward III heavily invested their wealth, therefore, not only in architecture and the arts but also in the creation of elegant parks and gardens.

Despite having only a limited selection of indigenous plants to work with, the earliest horticulturists were able to create the desired effect with the emphasis on pleasure rather than produce. Gardens were created enclosed by walls or trellises with climbing roses that provided much sought-after privacy away from the prying eyes of the household. Sweet smelling jasmine, honeysuckle and herbs masked any unsavoury odours from infrequent bathing and the garden soon became a fashionable place for private liaisons.

Sadly, no medieval gardens survive intact in Britain today but traces have been uncovered by archaeologists at Whittington Castle in Shropshire. These suggest that although contemporary illustrations by French and Flemish artists were

Warkworth Hermitage was allegedly carved from solid stone by a lover in penitence and grief.

often imaginary, allegorical works, the gardens depicted were based on actual late medieval layouts.

Some of the works of Christine de Pisan have been illustrated with lovers courting amongst ornamental trees and roses on a flowery mead or chamomile lawn, but it is the celebrated poem *Le Roman de la Rose* that gives us the most sumptuous image of the Garden of Pleasure. This thirteenth-century piece was one of the most widely read works in the French language and since French was for many years the official language of the English court, *The Romance of the Rose* was almost as important in England as it was on the continent. Although the walled garden that the dreaming narrator was invited to enter was a metaphorical one and his entire experience symbolic of sexual intercourse, *The Romance of the Rose* provides a valuable glimpse into late medieval attitudes to these alluring new spaces.

The complex origins of the maze can be traced back through the knotted designs of Celtic art, the swirling, circular motifs of prehistoric rock art and even the concentric plan of timbers at the Avebury Sanctuary. Mazes appeared on ancient coins from the Mediterranean kingdom of Crete and were made from pebbles on the shores of Sweden and Iceland. From the twelfth century onwards, the spiralling intricacies of the maze design enjoyed a renaissance.

In Europe, especially in France, maze designs were incorporated into ecclesiastical architecture at places like Chârtres Cathedral, signifying the Christian path to salvation, and now they resurfaced in the British landscape in late medieval gardens.

Naturally, the royal household was keen to keep up with continental trends and King Henry II was no exception. He had a beautiful mistress – the Fair Rosamond, daughter of Walter de Clifford – whom he installed in a dwelling 'of a wonderfull working, so that no man or woman might come to her, but if he were instructed by the king'. This labyrinthine home, 'wrought like unto a knotte in a garden, called a Maze', became known as Rosamond's Bower. According to legend, Queen Eleanor grew resentful of the king's attachment to his attractive young concubine. In his absence, Eleanor penetrated the maze where she offered Rosamond the choice of a sword or cup of poison. She chose the poison.

But here legend seems to have parted ways with history. Rosamond was, indeed, concubine to King Henry II but she was not murdered by Queen Eleanor. She retired, in fact, to Godstow nunnery near Oxford where she died around 1176 and was buried in a carved tomb draped with silken hangings in front of the high altar. The site of Rosamond's Bower survives on the north side of the lake at what is now Blenheim Palace, and here too is Rosamond's Well, a pool in which the beautiful concubine used to bathe. The term 'Rosamond's Bower' became widely used as a generic term for enclosed pleasure gardens, but her legendary loveliness is perhaps more lastingly commemorated by a rose, the crimson, pink and white *Rosa gallica versicolor*.

Although mazes were a feature of fashionable gardens across Europe, the turf maze was a phenomenon peculiar to the British landscape. In villages throughout England low, convoluted patterns were created in grass ranging in diameter from just five or six to nearly fifty metres. Julian's Bower, in the small village of Alkborough in South Humberside, is one of the most attractive and well-preserved examples.

On a grassy hillside that basks in the setting sun overlooking a confluence of the River Trent, lie the concentric, looping rings of a tightly formed English turf maze. The design is named after Julius, the son of Aeneas of Troy, a town whose walls were so constructed that the enemy, having entered the town, would not be able to find their way out again. Its raised pathway is worn by the treading of many feet in an ancient and symbolic pattern and although the church adopted this motif to signify the path of the soul to salvation its origins are deeply rooted in prehistoric rites associated with fertility. Indeed, until

'And the quaint mazes in the wanton green, for lack of tread, are indistinguishable . . .' – *A Midsummer Night's Dream*. Hilton is one of the few English turf mazes to have survived intact since the Middle Ages.

relatively recently games were held at Julian's Bower on May Eve, the pagan spring festival invoking fruitfulness in people, crops and animals. Fewer than ten medieval turf mazes survive in Britain. The village green at Hilton in Cambridgeshire hosts one of the best examples.

Labyrinthine patterns were flourishing in gardens of Italy and France formed of dense evergreen hedging such as yew and this fashion inevitably soon spread to Elizabethan England. Within the intricate curves and passages of a maze young couples could escape the observations of their chaperones and servants:

> And so with trees close set
> Was all the place, and hawthorn hedges knit
> That no one though he were near walking by
> Might there within scarce anyone espy.

As one historian put it: 'There was the conspiratorial fun of entering it; the laughing and jostling to find the centre; the gratifying discovery that there was no one else there . . . It was impossible not to be amorous in a maze.' As ever, royalty were at the cutting edge of hedge fashion: at Hever Castle in Kent, Henry VIII first set eyes upon Anne Boleyn, soon to become his second wife, and courted her, among other places, in the maze.

By the late medieval period gardens had become a fashionable and fundamental part of the landscape of polite British society. Landowners were abandoning dowdy strongholds in favour of architect-designed houses, and pleasure gardens were now an essential accessory for aspiring aristocrats. But continental influences ensured that discreet rose-covered trellises and intricate yew mazes would soon be discarded in favour of the licentious landscapes that would become the height of risqué vogue in post-medieval England.

Bolsover Castle in Derbyshire became one of the most intriguing and erotic households in seventeenth-century Britain.

CHAPTER SEVEN

Licentious Landscapes

THE ENGLISH ARE NATURALLY INCLINED TO PLEASURE, AS THERE IS NO
COUNTRIE WHEREIN THE GENTLEMEN AND LORDS HAVE SO MANY LARGE
PARKS . . . OR ALOT SO MUCH GROUND ABOUT THEIR HOUSES FOR
PLEASURE OF GARDENS.

FYNES THOMPSON

As increasing foreign trade brought growth to the nation's economy, the fortunes of some families also began to prosper. British aristocrats were keen to keep up with influences from Renaissance Europe, where classical culture was enjoying a widespread revival, expressing their wealth and taste in the latest architectural and garden designs. It was in this climate of educated decadence that certain spirited individuals indulged their love of classicism with occasionally startling results.

One of those was William Cavendish – a well-known patron of the arts. William's father, Charles Cavendish, had begun substantial alterations at the family home in 1613. Perched high on the edge of a rocky outcrop with expansive views to the west, the golden turreted walls of Bolsover Castle in Derbyshire dominate the skyline for miles around. With the help of a brilliant designer and stone mason, Robert Smythson, Charles envisioned the creation of a fantasy medieval castle but Bolsover would become one of the most intriguing – and erotic – households in seventeenth-century Britain.

William had inherited his father's passion for architecture, music and the arts and, just four years after building work began, he inherited the entire Bolsover estate. William was a devoted husband but he was also a diligent womaniser. His passion for women was rivalled only by his love of horses, and at Bolsover he indulged both with extravagant enthusiasm.

Overlooking the Venus Fountain in the Garden of Love, the Little Castle at Bolsover was designed for the indulgence of very personal pleasures.

Perhaps it was no coincidence that the Cavendish family crest portrayed an entwined serpent – an ancient symbol of sexual desire. Employing Robert Smythson's son John, William brought to fruition the vision of their fathers, incorporating new ideas from the continent and from the Italian-influenced work of Inigo Jones. Bolsover Castle was transformed into an elegant country home where William could play host to polite society. It was dominated by the Terrace Range – a suite of sumptuously furnished rooms with

Inside the Little Castle are murals of Elysium — a pagan heaven where the gods and goddesses of Ancient Greece cavort naked in scenes of orgiastic revelry.

Satyrs ride on the backs of mythical and immodest beasts.

views over the valley below – but his greatest achievement was the Little Castle.

In early seventeenth-century England, 'mock' medieval castles were the essence of high society fashion. Often more architecturally innovative than the main house, these were places where Jacobean aristocrats and a small party of friends could withdraw from the bustle of the household to re-live a past era of chivalry and romance. Though it stood on the site of a twelfth-century keep, the battlemented tower of the Little Castle at Bolsover was not for defence. Inspired by the Palazzo del Té in Italy – built by the Duke of Mantua for his mistress – it was designed, in a tradition of secret pleasure houses, entirely around the theme of love. Its sturdy walls also provided William with a place for the private indulgence of very personal pleasures.

The interior was sumptuously decorated with gilded panelling and wall hangings but it was the murals that earned the Little Castle its carnal reputation. The walls throughout are covered in richly painted scenes of seduction and temptation. The five senses are depicted in voluptuous sensuality, and upstairs, in a chamber modernly dubbed the 'Lesbian Room', brazen taffeta wall hangings frame fleshy maidens caressing one another in scenes of all-female eroticism. But the paintings were intended for

A copy of Giambolgna's 'Bathing Venus' in white Derbyshire stone surmounts the fountain in the Garden of Love.

more than visual delectation. An allegorical journey began at the main doorway in which William presented alternatives to physical gratification. To enter the Little Castle, it has been said, 'is to leave the everyday behind, and to enter a new world where everything has a hidden meaning'. An actual journey through three storeys of increasingly spiritual rooms reflected the contemporary neo-Platonist idea of the universe as a series of planes ascending to God through divine love. And at the top of the castle was a room adorned with cherubim and seraphim known as Heaven. But this is not the only chamber to open off William's bedroom. A doorway opposite leads into Elysium — a pagan heaven where the gods and goddesses of Ancient Greece cavort naked in an orgiastic scene of wine-drinking and love-making.

At points within the castle, tantalising glimpses are caught of the grounds below. Encapsulating both the medieval concept of the enclosed, secret garden and the Renaissance passion for outdoor statuary, the Garden of Love provided a fitting context for the libidinous Little Castle. From the confines of heady Elysium, a balcony looks directly out across the garden, at the centre of which is an octagonal sunken fountain designed to be viewed from above and surmounted by Venus herself.

Sketches outlining the original plan for the Venus Fountain show an array of naked women with jets of water issuing from every conceivable orifice. Remarkable for its own — or any other — time it is regrettable that this design was never realised. But William did commission a copy of Giambolgna's 'Bathing Venus' statue in Rome to be carved by local masons from brilliant white Derbyshire stone. From niches surrounding Venus's pedestal, classical busts of Roman emperors stare serenely but these are offset by a whole array of lustful creatures. Griffins squat on haunches displaying large and erect genitalia beside satyrs riding on the backs of similarly immodest beasts. These fantastical figures rest upon seat-like ledges, within the fountain, raising suspicions that these waters also tempted al fresco bathers.

By 1634 William's estate at Bolsover had, perhaps not surprisingly, aroused royal interest and in July of that year an extravagant entertainment was arranged here in honour of King Charles I and Queen Henrietta Maria. The writer Ben Jonson was commissioned to craft a masque, or musical drama entitled *Love's Welcome* to be performed at various locations within the castle grounds. In an unparalleled display of extravagance and ingenuity, a sumptuous feast, including peacocks and swans, descended from above by means of a mechanical device, 'set downe before them from the Cloudes'. The food was accompanied by verses spoken by two

Griffins squat on haunches displaying large and erect genitalia.

cupids who flattered, and described the love between King Charles and his queen as 'circular and perfect'. In this provocative setting, however, it seems unlikely that the proceedings remained so restrained for long.

The cost of hosting one of the most lavish entertainments of the time was over £15,000, and William was plunged into debt. Unlike his fortune, the Little Castle endured, almost untouched, as the most enchanting example of seventeenth-century fantasy and romantic folly. Its theme of the moral dilemma of physical lust versus divine love – or vice over virtue – was one that would influence the design of gardens for the next hundred years.

At the age of just twenty-one, Sir Richard Temple, fourth Baronet and later Viscount Cobham, found himself in possession of a vast area of rolling countryside just north of Buckingham. Through his transformation of a modest walled garden outside the village of Stowe into one of England's most elegant country estates, this young aristocrat became one of the greatest exponents of the eighteenth-century art of English landscape gardening.

Viscount Cobham worked with numerous visionary gardeners and architects, including Sir John Vanbrugh, Charles Bridgeman and Lancelot 'Capability' Brown, to create a garden that was as much a treat for the intellect as it was for the eye. In the January 1710 issue of *Tatler*, an article appeared in which Joseph Addison recounted an allegorical dream staged in a symbolic setting of woods, pathways and temples. This may have been the inspiration for the grounds at Stowe in which the architectural components, planting, even the vistas, alluded to mythological narratives and where metaphor, symbol and pun combined to elicit specific responses from the onlooker and reflected Cobham's own values and political views.

The Viscount was descended from a family line of Whigs who, in the previous century had striven for the establishment of a constitutional monarchy and political freedom in Britain. He himself was a fervent supporter of liberalism and of a moral code he saw embodied in the classical culture of ancient Greece. The Stowe gardens were divided into two halves, east and west. The eastern side, now the more famous, is where his designs commented, often very personally, upon national politics and its contemporary characters. The western side, which recently has received less attention by landscape historians, was all about Cobham's attitudes to personal relationships – in particular sex.

Here, the temples and monuments shared the common theme of Love, but this was not a garden about idealised romanticism. In what may seem like social psychotherapy on a monumental scale, the

Classical busts of Nero, an infamously debauched emperor, and the adulteress Cleopatra stand in niches within the Venus Temple at Stowe.

classical references at Stowe raised issues such as unrequited yearning, illicit or adulterous unions and bestial passion.

Upon entering the gardens by the Bell Gate, visitors were presented with a magnificent view across the Octagon Lake and up sweeping grassed slopes to the grandeur of the Palladian house. To the left of the gate stood two Lake Pavilions, the rear walls of which were once elaborately painted with scenes from the Italian opera *Pastor Fido*. Here, two classical tales of unrequited love are depicted: that of the nymph Dorinda and Sylvio the hunter, and that of Amarillis who rejected the advances of Myrtillo. On lawns in front of the pavilions statuesque satyrs cavorted with a

The Rotondo at Stowe, designed by Vanbrugh, is known as one of Lord Cobham's 'most solemnly beautiful and elegant' temples.

goddess of love but also the patroness of gardens. At Stowe she was venerated in a magnificent temple of Helmdon limestone, set back from the edge of Eleven Acre Lake and inscribed with the words 'Veneri Hortensi', 'to Venus of the Garden'. Although the source of the design is a mystery, a few fragments remain of the paintings that once adorned the walls and ceiling inside the temple and their meaning is well understood.

Scenes by the Venetian artist Francesco Sleter were taken from the lines in Spenser's *Faerie Queen* in which Malbecco and Hellinore's story of adultery and seduction is told. These allegorical murals are accompanied by an inscription in Latin translating as:

Let him love, who never lov'd before;
Let him who always lov'd, now love the more.

The temple, it appears, was conveniently furnished with a 'pleasuring sopha' for the purpose.

The original presence, outside Venus's Temple, of lead statues of the brothers Cain and Abel seems, at first, somewhat inappropriate. Their significance here may be explained, though, in the lines of Samuel Boyse's poem 'The Triumph of Nature' written in 1742:

Thy temple, beauteous Venus, we survey'd;
Before, fit emblem of the lover's view,

dancing Venus – characters that were to feature highly in the adventure through Cobham's sexual wonderland.

The creative use of mythology and ancient history to inspire particular feelings in visitors would not have been wasted on a genteel audience with a classical education. Visitors would have been well aware, for example, that Venus was not only the

Stand the first foes which nature ever knew;
Fit emblem, goddess, of thy cruel pow'r,
Which oft has bath'd the warring world in gore;
Has smil'd to set the dearest friends at strife,
And make the brother snatch the brother's life:
Yet mild at first, thy savage yoke appears,
And like this scene a beauteous prospect wears;
For scenes like this, thy fatal flame inspire,
Unnerve the soul – and kindle soft desire!

This ability of Venus to promote sexual jealousy among mortals is further emphasised by the busts of four prominent Romans that adorn the portico niches. Nero, an infamously debauched Emperor, appears at the side of Cleopatra, the adulterer who seduced both Caesar and Marc Antony. In contrast, the Emperor Vespasian and Faustina, his devoted wife, are, it seems, the embodiment of intellect and virtue – though it is not clear which of these opposing paths Viscount Cobham was advocating.

Another folly which once stood in the grounds, St Augustine's Cave, has not survived the passing of time. Described as 'a cell form'd of Moss and Roots of Trees interwoven, with a straw Couch in the Inside', this organic thatched structure was built along an unlikely amorous theme. It apparently contained three lewd inscriptions in 'Monkish Latin Verse' which chronicled the hermit-saint's attempts

Inside the Rotondo at Stowe stands an exquisite gilded statue of the Venus de Medici.

175

to conquer his lustful thoughts, leading one to suspect that the couch in this 'cave' had a purpose other than seated prayer.

The Temple of Bacchus, a simple brick-pedimented structure designed by Vanbrugh, was at one time regarded as one of the finest buildings at Stowe. It was dedicated to Bacchus – god of wine, drunkenness and lechery – and scenes by Joseph Nollekens entitled 'Revels of Bacchus' once adorned the interior. Sadly, in an act reminiscent of the iconoclastic destruction at Avebury stone circle, the Temple was torn down in 1926 to be replaced with a chapel. This may have been a coincidental move but it is tempting to infer conclusions about how moral priorities had changed by the early twentieth century.

But it is another of Vanbrugh's architectural works that is known today as 'the most solemnly beautiful and eloquent of Lord Cobham's temples'. The Rotondo is a magnificent circular structure with open sides formed of eight towering columns. Inside the temple, like a caged exotic bird, stands an exquisite gilded statue of the Venus de Medici. Situated on a terrace high above the waters of Eleven Acre Lake, the Rotondo once formed the central focus of the Garden of Love. A bird's eye view of the park drawn in 1719 shows a series of walkways and planted avenues converging on the golden Venus. Clearly, she was originally an integral part of Cobham's open-air

discourse on the subject of love, a feature noted by Gilbert West in his poem on the Stowe garden:

Shift now the closer Scene: and view around,
With various beauties the wide Landskip
crown'd . . .
Lo! In the Centre of this beauteous Scene,
Glitters beneath her Dome the Cyprian Queen.

But it was not only to allegorical passion that the grounds at Stowe played host. Dido's Cave is a rustic sandstone grotto with a rough facade of oolitic limestone, now almost submerged by the encroaching shrubbery. Its interior was once painted with scenes recalling the story of Queen Dido of Carthage and her lover Aeneas, as told in Virgil's *Aeneid*. While out hunting, the pair sought shelter from a storm in a cave, in which their love was consummated, but this mythological reference was employed only after a legendary incident on the estate.

The local vicar, it is said, while playing bowls one day, was apparently smitten with a young lady he saw playing on a nearby swing. Seized by the sensation to which he is said to have given his name, the Reverend Rand pursued the alarmed girl, who took refuge in what she mistakenly thought was a safe hiding place. The secretive nature of the grotto did not work to her advantage, however, and within sight of the golden

Dido's Cave was decorated with mythological scenes of love-making after an alleged incident on the estate.

goddess of love, the vicar caught up with her, with predictable consequences. The interior is now a delicate and eclectic montage of shells and coral, quartz, amethyst and sherds of mirror as the result of a later fashion for shell grottoes and the efforts of the Marchioness of Buckingham in 1781. In a curiously Oedipal gesture her son, the first Duke, made Dido's Cave, with all its carnal connotations, a memorial to the Marchioness.

The two areas of the gardens at Stowe have traditionally been viewed as conceptually separate: that to the west being devoted to the theme of love

Medmenham Abbey on the banks of the River Thames where 'a thousand kisses of fire were given, and a thousand others returned'.

and the eastern landscape being dedicated to political comment. But perhaps, in reality, this division is not so straightforward.

Cobham was a member of a group known as the Kit Cat Club. This fraternity of Whigs included many of his friends and drinking companions such as Sir John Vanbrugh and the dramatist William Congreve. These men would have been aware of the contemporary debate on women's rights. It has been suggested that the Whig philosopher, John Locke, 'was amongst the first to sense the inherent contradiction in a "liberalism" based on the natural freedom of mankind, which afforded to women no greater freedom than allowed by patriarchalism'. Cobham's eastern garden might therefore be regarded as a discourse not only on love but also on the wider issue of sexual politics.

The landscape gardens at Stowe, described by Alexander Pope as 'a work to wonder at', were to influence garden design around the world. The ebb of the cultural tide was, for a while, reversed as in France a fashion rapidly spread for 'jardins anglais' with elements from Stowe being used at the Petit Trianon at the royal palace of Versailles. Thomas Jefferson was so impressed during his visit in 1786 that he commissioned similar work at his home in Monticello, but the greatest admirer was perhaps Empress Catherine the Great of Russia. She sent her head gardener to England to be immersed in a style that he later created for the Empress in her home country. A little closer to home, at the other end of the county, the Stowe gardens were being not copied but parodied by one of Cobham's arch enemies, the infamous rake Sir Francis Dashwood.

Less than forty miles from London, in the heart of the Chiltern hills, Dashwood created at West Wycombe Park a landscape of sexual allusion that would become one of the most admired, and certainly the most scandalous, of eighteenth-century gardens. But it was six miles away, at Medmenham Abbey on the River Thames near Marlow, that infamy first arose surrounding the orgiastic meetings of the Hell-Fire Club.

As a young man Dashwood had spent many years abroad on an extended version of the fashionable Grand Tour. During prolonged stays in places as culturally diverse as Italy and the Ottoman Empire he not only indulged an existing penchant for high living and heavy drinking but also cultivated a genuine interest in architecture and the arts. In the mid-1700s Dashwood formed a club in which all his most passionate interests could be indulged.

Originally known as the Order of the Knights of Saint Francis of Medmenham it comprised, in the words of one member, 'a set of worthy, jolly fellows, happy disciples of Venus and Bacchus, [who] got together occasionally to celebrate woman in wine and to give more zest to the festive meeting, they plucked every luxurious idea from the ancients and enriched their own modern pleasures with the tradition of classic luxury'. Knights of Saint Francis they may have been, but the meetings were anything but pious.

Aristocrats, members of Parliament, and even an Archbishop of Canterbury were among Dashwood's closest friends and political acquaintances invited to join an elite circle of 'monks' – though vows of celibacy, it seems, were definitely not a requirement. Initial meetings were held in the Vulture Inn in the City of London and the George Tavern at West Wycombe, but it soon became clear that a secluded venue was needed for the revelry of Dashwood's boisterous group. The ruined twelfth-century Cistercian abbey, in a grove of trees some distance from the road, accessible by boat from the River Thames, was the perfect location; the move to more private quarters perhaps not only facilitated but encouraged the profane scenes that would unfold.

Medmenham Abbey was transformed with the addition of a gothic cloister and tower. The inscription 'Fay ce que voudras' or 'Do whatever you will' over the entrance no doubt set the tone of a building in which a Roman room was adorned with erotic paintings copied from ancient frescoes. The library contained not only books on architecture, literature and art but also perhaps one of the most complete pornographic collections in England.

Members were sworn to secrecy regarding the agenda of their meetings so it is difficult to discern with certainty what went on within the confines of the Abbey. Rumours circulated of satanic worship and Black Mass being celebrated over the naked bodies of aristocratic ladies – including one Lady Montagu Wortley, mother-in-law of one of the mock friars. Although there is absolutely no evidence linking the group with occult practices, mock religious rites do seem to have been performed in which Venus, the goddess of love, and Bacchus, the god of wine, were the unconventional subjects of worship. Ladies were admitted to the meetings for the purposes of pleasure. Prostitutes were shipped in barges up the River Thames from London to act as 'nuns'; local girls were sometimes invited to attend and even ladies of society took part, their identities protected by the adoption of a masquerade.

The 'monks' wore white costumes while the 'Abbot' was distinguishable in red fur-trimmed garb. He also had first choice of the ladies present at each gathering. Naked girls served feasts of fine food and wine. Pages from a surviving Cellar Book show that a considerable amount of wine and port was imbibed and accounts record a silversmith being commissioned to craft silver goblets for the group in

the shape of women's breasts. Obscene songs and toasts, it seems, were the norm but some accounts suggest that bawdier evenings occasionally evolved into scenes of orgiastic revelry and sumptuously furnished 'cells' were provided for those 'monks' who wished to make their devotions to Venus in private. Guests could also be admitted to the meetings and it is thought that Benjamin Franklin and Charles Wesley, preacher and founder of the Methodists, although not fully paid up members, both attended evenings hosted by the society.

Around Medmenham Abbey, Dashwood created a 'Garden of Lust'. Marble pillars were erected here and carved with libidinous inscriptions like boastful graffiti in French and Latin: 'In this place a thousand kisses of fire given and a thousand others returned' and 'Here the vanquished naiad overcame the conquering satyr'. A series of erotic figurines, sensuously disporting in indecent poses graced the Abbey gardens, and at the entrance to Trophonious' Cave was a statue of Venus bending over to pull a thorn out of her foot. Just beyond her exposed rear was the inscription: 'Here is the place where the way divided into two: this on the right is our route to heaven; but the left-hand path exacts punishment from the wicked and sends them to pitiless Hell.' But inside the cave was a mossy couch and the exhortation: 'Go into action, you youngsters; put

The Temple of Venus erected by Sir Francis Dashwood at his West Wycombe home.

everything you've got into it together, both of you; let not the doves outdo your cooings, nor ivy your embraces, nor oysters your kisses.' Clearly the threat of spiritual repercussions was taken with as much levity as the rest of the entertainment.

Not surprisingly Sir Francis's 'monks' became the subject of considerable scandal and were eventually forced to withdraw from Medmenham. The Abbey was re-styled by the Victorians but, although the erotic follies have disappeared, the fine Georgian

Mercury surmounts the narrow entrance to the Venus Parlour at West Wycombe.

colonnade and tower still cast their elegant reflection in the River Thames. With a little imagination, it is possible to envisage boats full of masquerading revellers in wigs, costumes and high spirits pulling up alongside the private moorings in expectation of an outrageous evening's entertainment.

At his family home of West Wycombe, Dashwood had also been busy. Over twenty hectares of lawns, woods and paths were remodelled to a Rococo design drawn up by Sir Francis and the landscape architect Maurice-Louis Jolivet. The River Wye was dammed to create a series of serpentine rills that flowed into a swan-shaped lake. A Music Temple, designed by William Revett and reachable only by boat, was built on one of three islands in the lake to function as a theatrical setting for *fêtes champêtres*. The parterres and pathways of the new garden were laid out in the daringly evocative form of a naked woman. Together the gardens and lake evoked the myth of Leda, raped by Zeus in the form of a swan.

Numerous follies and gazebos were constructed in secluded spots for rest during perambulation of the park – or perhaps a little privacy. In the middle of this landscape Dashwood erected the Temple of Venus, a folly in a woodland clearing dedicated to the goddess of love. A statue of Venus, like her gilded counterpart at Stowe, stands within a rotunda of twelve ionic columns. The rotunda sits atop a grassy mound over the entrance to the temple's grotto, known as Venus's Parlour. The concept of the Venus Mound at the centre of the evocative landscape form was one that was to be later picked up by Victorian writers:

> What a perfect forest overshadowed it, and how divine were the slopes of that glorious hill, the perfect little mountain, which led down the sweet descent to the deep vale between her thighs, and ended in that glowing grotto in which love delighted to hide his blushing head and shed hot tears of exulting joy.

The symbolism at play here is hardly subtle yet it was originally underlined further by the inclusion of an embracing circle of erotic statues in front of the opening to the grotto. Jolivet's original designs show monkeys, a medieval symbol of lust, cavorting amongst the alcoves of the flint façade but these may never have been added. The Temple of Venus seen by modern visitors to West Wycombe was recreated by Quinlan Terry in 1982; although the erotic statues are no longer in place it is quite possible to appreciate the effect desired by Dashwood in the eighteenth century. The responses elicited by this immodest shrine were no doubt varied then, as they would be today – if the garden's meaning were more widely realised. And looking at the Venus Mound, with its rounded grassy

The Temple of Apollo at West Wycombe is inscribed with the motto of the Hell-Fire Club.

slopes, its dark aperture and subterranean chamber, one is struck by the profound resemblance to prehistoric burial mounds – the womb of Mother Earth.

A consort to Venus was introduced to the gardens in the form of Apollo Belvedere. The Temple of Apollo beyond the south front of the house is an elegant archway with mosaic flooring, generally attributed to the architect John Donowell. A statue of the classical god graces an alcove beyond, attended by small stonework cupids. The entablature above the arch is inscribed with the motto of the Hell-Fire Club – 'Liberati Amici Liaeq(ue) Sac(rum)', 'Sacred to Liberty and Friendship' and meetings of the society were reputed to have convened here on occasions.

West Wycombe house was remodelled in eighteenth-century Palladian style but it was never completed as a single entity by one architect. The façades of the house instead represent a series of piecemeal alterations producing four conceptually separate fronts, the most dramatic of which is the West Portico – an entrance which also served as the Temple of Bacchus. Designed by William Revett this portico represented the first reproduction of a Greek temple in England and its creation established Dashwood as a pioneer of neo-classicism. William Hannan was commissioned to paint three frescoes on the ceiling: of Selene in her Chariot of the Night, of a Bacchic Procession, and of Bacchus and Ariadne after the ruined Temple of Bacchus at Teos near Smyrna.

A large lead statue of Bacchus was erected on a pedestal within the portico and a dedication ceremony was held for the temple in September 1771. Bacchanals, priests, priestesses, satyrs, fauns and a Pan, all wreathed with vine leaves, ivy and oak, formed a procession led by the High Priest (certainly Sir Francis himself). The statue of Bacchus was addressed in a sensual invocation with drinking and singing and the assembly 'having finished the sacrifice proceeded through the groves to a Tent pitched at the head of the lake where the paeans and libations were repeated'. The 'devotees' of this intemperate god then adjourned to a decorated barge on the lake where they 'performed various ceremonies', but here the writer leaves us on the lakeside to wonder at the details of scenes that unfolded on the boat between the intoxicated satyrs and fauns.

In an altogether worldlier sphere, hardcore was needed in 1748 for the construction of a new road between High Wycombe and West Wycombe. An open cast quarry already existed on the slopes of West Wycombe Hill but Dashwood saw an opportunity to create a subterranean folly. Many tonnes of chalk were removed as a network of tunnels was excavated quarter of a mile beneath the hill. Entered through an impressive gothic flint-work façade, the arch-roofed

The West Wycombe caves are entered through an impressive gothic flint-work façade.

passages lead deep underground. Their ways divide and rejoin in a labyrinthine pattern that clearly had a purpose other than as a simple source for road-building material.

At one point the tunnel opens into a cathedral-like vault known as the Banquet Hall and a River Styx, complete with faux stalactites, is crossed before reaching the Inner Temple. It is thought that Sir Francis played host to his elite society members here after their retreat from Medmenham; the sound of merry-making must have echoed through the eerie chambers at the inaugural party at the opening of the caves. The spirit of the group had evidently not been subdued as legend states that this is where many

185

'Wycombe wenches lost the last vestiges of their innocence' deep underground in the maze of tunnels and chambers.

'Wycombe wenches lost the last vestiges of their innocence'.

Many metres above the caves, on the top of West Wycombe Hill, Dashwood remodelled a ruinous medieval church but even this was not spared the libertine touch of one of the eighteenth-century's most notorious hedonists. The interior of St Lawrence's Church was lavishly decorated with rich Rococo plasterwork, classical friezes in the style of Robert Wood's 'Ruins of Palmyra' and the altar was covered in Spanish leather. Five doves are depicted on the font, one of which is in danger of being devoured by a serpent that winds up the font's shaft. This could be a reference to Jesus' advice to his disciples: 'be ye

From the golden ball on St Lawrence's Church, four round windows looked down over Dashwood's erotic gardens.

therefore wise as serpents, and harmless as doves' or it could be a more lascivious image of sexual appetite encroaching on the innocent.

But the crowning glory of St Lawrence's Church, and Dashwood's pièce de résistance, was a shimmering golden ball. Visible from the house and almost every point within the grounds, this gilded sphere was hoisted to the top of the tower in 1751. A trap door cut in the lower half of the ball swung down to allow an intimate group access to a rather cramped interior. Despite its diminutive status as a venue, the golden ball was described as being 'for the celebration not of devotional but of convivial rites', John Wilkes adding wryly that 'it is the best globe tavern I was ever

The lakeside Pantheon was principal amongst the temples at Stourhead.

in'. Four rounded windows in the ball look down onto the park and perhaps it was from here that the fabled naked woman in the garden design could be privately appreciated.

As Viscount Cobham of Stowe joined the opposition to the government in which Dashwood was a minister, the rivalry between the two men grew. In a trend that seems quite odd to modern minds, the political tensions of the City of London were played out in symbolism in the grounds of their respective country estates. Perhaps Dashwood was commenting on the over-zealousness of Cobham's personal sexual politics when he created a deliberately frivolous and self-indulgent landscape. Sadly, many of the most explicit components of the erotic gardens were erased by the succeeding generation of Dashwoods but enough traces survive to realise that the irrepressible character of Sir Francis left an enduring mark on the English countryside. The landscape features of both Stowe and West Wycombe were to influence greatly the design of other contemporary gardens. The theme of Venus, in particular, was soon being emulated in several fashionable estates.

Castle Howard near York is an awe-inspiring edifice of baroque and Palladian grandeur and, undoubtedly, one of Britain's finest country houses. Here, Vanbrugh was responsible for the Temple of Diana, known today

'Venus of the beautiful buttocks' stands in a pedimented niche within the Pantheon at Stourhead.

The choice is presented at
Stourhead between the
rocky uphill path of virtue
or the easy path of
pleasure and vice.

as the Temple of the Four Winds. This august structure, inspired by Palladio's Villa Rotonda in Vicenza, sits at the east end of a sweeping terrace that was the high street of the now vanished medieval village of Henderskelfe.

Nicholas Hawksmoor designed a Temple of Venus a quarter of a mile to the north but still in sight of Vanbrugh's creation. Far from being simply another display of classicism this open, columned rotunda with its charming statue of Venus de Medici symbolised a daring comment on the sexual morals of the time. The goddess Diana, protector of children, representing the security of motherhood and home, had been challenged by the arrival of a nubile seductress, the implied reference being perhaps the temptation of free love over the loyalty of the marital relationship. But Diana need not have worried. In the 1940s Castle Howard's resident agent instructed the head forester to fell a tree on to Venus's unstable rotunda, an act that razed it to the ground.

Today, the gardens at Stourhead in Wiltshire are a haven of elegance and beauty. Classical temples framed by heavy-headed rhododendrons are reflected in the waters of a lake that was the inspiration, mainly, of one man – Henry Hoare II.

As a young man, Hoare, like Dashwood of West Wycombe, had spent many months in Italy. Now he strove to create the perfect garden – a poetic landscape with orchestrated views and grand buildings reminiscent of classical and Renaissance Rome. Unlike other English country estates, the house at Stourhead lay some distance from the site of his proposed paradise so Hoare was not restricted by considering viewpoints either to or from the house. Two steep hills met at Six Bottom Wells where springs issued from the ground forming the head of the River Stour. Hoare had these dammed to create a magnificent lake around which he added temples and trees in a place that, indeed, became known as Paradise.

Principal among the temples was the Pantheon. Modelled directly on the original in Rome Hoare's Pantheon formed both the visual and symbolic focus of the garden. The temple was impressively designed with Corinthian columns and a huge domed rotunda. Its interior hosted an array of classical gods and goddesses including the passion of his youth, the goddess Diana. But it is the quirky statues outside that are perhaps most appealing.

In pedimented niches on either side of the vestibule are figures of Bacchus and the Venus Callipygos, 'Venus of the beautiful buttocks'. This figure of Venus recalls the story of two sisters. Unable to agree upon who had the lovelier behind, the girls asked the opinion of a passing young man. He duly picked his favourite bottom and was rewarded with an offer of marriage from the winning sister, to which he readily conceded. In honourable fashion, however, the consolation prize for the owner of the rejected rump was to be wed to the young man's brother.

Hanging among the oil paintings in Hoare's impressive collection at Stourhead is Poussin's 'Choice of Hercules'. A naked, heroic god is depicted faced with the choice between the rocky uphill path of virtue or the easy path of pleasure and vice embodied in two maidens of respectively virtuous and immodest appearance. In the gardens at Stourhead, this choice is metaphorically translated into a point where the path divides to follow either a gentle lakeside stroll or an arduous ascent through a winding, rocky ravine. This moral dilemma was a popular eighteenth-century preoccupation and one that enthusiastic Protestants, such as Hoare, were particularly keen on.

On the opposite side of the lake, a similar ravine leads down to a shady aquamarine grotto that Hoare referred to as 'the temple of the nymph'. Fringed with ferns, this circular domed chamber has the chill, echoing atmosphere of a chapel but the constant trickle of water dispels any reverential silence. The cool vault, of 'rustic' local limestone and tufa imported from Italy, has a floor formed from thousands of pebbles set in concentric rings. Light filters in through an aperture in the roof to illuminate the pure white statue of a water nymph reclining on a

mossy plinth. Based upon a famous figurine of Ariadne in the Belvedere Gardens of the Vatican, her appearance is more modest than many pictorial depictions of these aquatic maidens.

But classical associations to this nymph are tinged with eroticism since Ariadne was the bride of Dionysus, the god of fertility. Because she wears a serpent bracelet, the figure in the Vatican was thought by some to be Cleopatra. Horace Walpole referred to this porcelain beauty as 'Cleopatra without the asp' but he was not the only man to be drawn to the water by this silent Siren. George Elliott wrote that she 'lies in the marble voluptuousness of her beauty, the drapery folding around her with a petal-like ease and tenderness'. Lines from a fifteenth century poem translated by Alexander Pope are inscribed in letters arcing around her pool:

> Nymph of the Grot, these sacred springs I keep
> And to the murmur of these waters sleep.
> Ah spare my slumbers, gently tread the cave,
> And drink in silence or in silence lave.

The word 'lave' was an invitation to bathe in the pool and even Hoare, it seems, allowed himself to be seduced. During a hot summer in 1762, he evidently took to bathing in the pool, exclaiming, 'A souse in that delicious bath and grot, fill'd with fresh magic, is

Inside Stourhead's
pebble grotto, a water
nymph 'lies in the
marble voluptuousness
of her beauty'.

Ranelagh Park: London's pleasure gardens acquired a reputation as places where 'a young lady's virtue came under threat'.

Asiatic luxury.'

In the eighteenth century, gentlemen's clubs gained notorious popularity. Like landscaped gardens, they were a curious mixture of hedonistic indulgence and serious political comment and provided a progressive environment in which like-minded individuals could socialise freely, unconstrained by the bounds of family or profession. Some of these societies were merely raucous but others were 'fervently libertine'.

At Anstruther, a small coastal town on the northern shore of the Firth of Forth, a group known as the Beggar's Benison would rival the Hell-Fire Club in scandal and intrigue. Dedicated to 'the convivial celebration of male sexuality' the group was founded by such upstanding members of society as customs officials and wealthy local merchants. By the end of the century, groups had also formed in Glasgow and Edinburgh and the list of subscribers had swelled to include clergy and aristocrats; even King George IV was granted honorary membership.

Meeting in a ruined castle, the Beggar's Benison did not indulge in the orgiastic activities of the Knights of Sir Francis. No doubt they dined and drank, accompanied by obscene songs and indelicate toasts but their interest in matters of sex was a genuinely earnest one. Educational lectures would be heard on oddly diverse matters, such as menstruation in fish, and the club held a healthy stock of pornography. Naked posturing girls would occasionally provide a diversion but the main preoccupation of the club was ritual masturbation.

Members of the group were strongly opposed to the warnings given by early eighteenth-century physicians of the threats to health and society posed by onanism. In an act that was not homosexual but political, these men defied convention by doing in public what was being discouraged even in private. As one writer described, 'Shameless "frigging" was an expression of intellectual freedom.' The Beggar's Benison symbol was, not surprisingly, a phallus, from which a small bag was suspended and the club motto read 'May prick nor purse ne'er fail you'. Relics from the group include a seal bearing this emblem and a small snuffbox that was donated by George IV containing the pubic hair of one of his mistresses. Despite this celebrity support, the group was temporarily disbanded. When it later reformed, meetings were held not at the ruined castle but on Anstruther shore at dawn.

At the same time in London, landscape architects such as Charles Bridgeman were turning their talents to creating pleasure grounds in the heart of the city. Public parks were soon adopted by members of high society as the place to be seen, though several also acquired a reputation as places 'where a young lady's virtue came under serious threat'.

Tree-lined promenades combined with ornamental fountains and cascades to produce an atmosphere that must have been a delightful contrast to the city streets, but the winding paths and shaded alleys were perhaps appreciated more as an opportunity for flirtations and seductions. In Tom Brown's 'Amusements Serious and Comical' of 1700, he described a place where 'both sexes meet and mutually serve one another as guides to lose their way; and the windings and turnings in the little wildernesses are so intricate that the most experienced mothers have often lost themselves in looking for their daughters'. And when Sir Roger de Coverley considered the 'fragrancy of the walks and the bowers with choirs of birds' he likened the grounds to 'a kind of Mahometan paradise'. Little wonder, then, that these gardens became famed for their aphrodisiac appeal.

There were three main pleasure grounds open to the public at the time, of which Ranelagh was undoubtedly the grandest. Sited on the north bank of the River Thames near Chelsea Bridge, it was said that here 'you can't set your foot without treading on a Prince or a Duke'. The small gardens were exquisitely designed with an ornamental lake and Chinese pagoda, the whole being dominated by a rotunda from

St James's Park near Buckingham Palace
was the scene of naked races and
bathing.

which music from an orchestra spilled out.

Ranelagh was fashionable with the elite of London's
society and it was here that a young continental
adventurer was offered a lift in a lady's carriage. By
the end of the ride the two were on considerably
more intimate terms. Several days later he was
somewhat bemused to meet the same lady at the
house of a mutual friend. When she showed no sign of
recognising him, the young man reminded her of their
meeting but was told, 'A frolic does not constitute an
introduction.' This gallant, who marvelled at the way
Englishwomen allowed themselves to be 'thus

vigorously wooed first and introduced afterwards', was named Casanova.

On the other side of the Thames, the pleasure grounds of Vauxhall were the most fashionable of the three. In a wonderland of unprecedented splendour, illuminated fountains and cascades were interspersed with mock romantic ruins. An account written in 1801 recalled: 'For beauty of situation and variety of elegant scenes, these gardens cannot be surpassed by any pleasure ground in the Kingdom . . . A great number of small, delightful groves, and charming lawns, intersected by serpentine walks, which at every turn meet with sweet shady bowers, furnished with handsome seats, some canopied by nature, others by art.' In its heyday twenty thousand people would flock to the park for nightime entertainments including circuses, theatres and hot-air balloon ascents.

Routes through the grounds with quixotic names such as the Dark Walk and Lover's Walk were popular venues for rendezvous, but these shady bowers soon acquired an even shadier reputation. Brothels grew up in the surrounding streets including the graphically named Slut's Hole in the road now known as Fitzalan Street. But perhaps the gardens most steeped in sexual intrigue were those at Marylebone. On fine summer evenings, finely dressed couples strolled in the park, entertained by singers on an open-air stage but, once the sun had set, the park became a hotbed of iniquity and no respectable members of society would be seen in Marylebone Gardens after dark.

St James's Park, originally created as a deer park for King Henry VIII, was the first Royal Park to open to the public. With Buckingham Palace to the west and the elegant skyline of Whitehall to the east, this attractive garden provided some of the most romantic views to be seen in London. An expanse of water known as the Canal extended throughout, flanked by the curves of winding paths and landscaped shrubberies. Though once the playground of high society, St James's Park, like the other London pleasure grounds, gradually sank into disreputability. Naked races and bathing in the Canal were amongst the more wholesome of the 'indecent practices' that took place in a park that eventually became the haunt of 'common prostitutes and soldiers'.

A fashionable crowd still flirted on The Mall, which lined the north side of St James's Park. This area gained notoriety as a high class pick-up spot and it was here that a dashing but hard-up aristocrat named Sir Francis Blake Delaval tricked a wealthy heiress into marrying him. Sir Francis's friend and sidekick, the actor Samuel Foote, while posing as a fortune-teller, had previously persuaded Rhoda Apreece that she was destined to meet her beau on The Mall, which is where Delaval contrived to seduce her. This rakish nobleman also frequented the shadier of London's

At Seaton Delaval Hall, partitions between bedrooms could be raised to expose surprised guests to one another in a state of undress.

parks and it was in Marylebone Gardens that he persuaded a young singer to become his mistress. Sir Francis's penchant for simultaneous liaisons was one that had enduring consequences at his country house in Northumberland.

Seaton Delaval Hall presents a grim face towards Scotland and the salt-laden wind as it whips inland off the North Sea. When Sir John Vanbrugh visited the old family residence in 1721, a storm was raging across this wild and romantic shore. Perhaps it was the tempest that inspired him to create what is often regarded as his architectural masterpiece but the magnificently brooding, dark, grey walls with their forbidding towers and columns would host a history of tragedy and lust to rival any *Wuthering Heights*.

Admiral George Delaval, who commissioned Vanbrugh's services, died in a riding accident – one of several deaths that were the result, it was said, of a

Starlight Castle was built in a single day by Sir Francis Delaval as a wager to house one of his many mistresses.

Mount Mapas, on the outskirts of Dublin, belongs to a genre of undeniably phallic monument.

curse placed on the family. The estate subsequently passed to Sir Francis, who squandered his inherited wealth in London on women of dubious reputation and on lavish parties at Seaton Delaval. With a reputation for 'gaiety, generosity and brilliance' this notorious Lothario hosted extravagant banquets for up to four thousand guests at a time in the draughty baroque hall. The gardens at such times were described as a 'fairyland of lights and beauty and music; with floating throngs of gay and lovely creatures that were ready to rush into the most extraordinary frolics and scenes of mischief imaginable'.

The backdrop to this sylvan stage was the west wing of the house, likened to the enchanted castle in Claude's painting of 'Psyche dismissed from the Castle of Eros'. And when the guests finally retired to bed another surprise lay in store. Sir Francis, well known for his practical jokes, had the walls of the upper hall rigged with pulleys and ropes. Upon his command – probably just long enough after people got out of their clothes and into more compromising positions – the partitions between bedrooms were raised, exposing his guests to one another in whatever state they were found.

At various times Sir Francis provided accommodation on the estate for several of his mistresses – at a discreet distance from the family home. When faced with the problem of having to house his latest sexual conquest he sought the confidence of one of his trusted friends. Samuel Foote, while acknowledging the need for a residence, lamented that a castle could not be built in one day. In characteristically brash response, Delaval set a wager of one hundred guineas that he could do just that. So preparations were made and an army of workmen drafted in for the challenge. After working through the night the picturesque Starlight Castle was constructed on a grassy knoll overlooking the valley of Holywell Dene. The remains of that castle still stand today and, although wild flowers now grow between the blocks of stone, its bold arches endure as a monument to one of that century's most infamous lovers.

Monuments of impressive elevation became something of an obsession in the eighteenth century. Amongst the breast-shaped parterres, the classical allusions to extra-marital love and the many secluded follies, a type of garden feature was making an appearance that was curiously reminiscent of the prehistoric standing stone or the spire of St Illtud's Church on Caldey Island.

Mount Mapas, on the outskirts of Dublin, belongs to a genre of undeniably phallic monument. Fashionably erected on the summit of Killiney Hill in 1792 in honour of John Mapas, the structure was clearly intended to impress. Such phallic memorials are found ubiquitously throughout the British Isles, many, like Mount Mapas, engraved with names and dates in a posthumous affirmation of virility even in death.

On the other side of the Irish Sea three towering monuments are synonymous with the sexual eccentricity of one obsessive man. William Beckford, a spoilt and lonely child, had become a millionaire at the age of nine and was the wealthiest young man in England. The family fortune had been built on Jamaican sugar plantations and inheriting it allowed him the freedom to indulge a love for created beauty. William also indulged his love for the son of Viscount Courtenay and was caught *in flagrante* by the butler. Sodomy, in the eighteenth century, was a capital offence and any hopes of social position were dashed. As a young man, Beckford adored exotic objets d'art that hinted at a mysterious world beyond the cloying conventionalities of his social set. He surrounded himself with Islamic, medieval and oriental impedimenta that softened the interface between his own environment and what he saw as 'the coarse, unpoetic tenor of the present disenchanting period'.

As a true Romantic, Beckford was nothing if not passionate. He abhorred the polite and mediocre tastes of the rising mercantile classes, choosing to champion instead the rights of animals and of the working man. And he was also deeply sexual.

Fonthill House, a Palladian mansion just west of Salisbury in Wiltshire, was known as Fonthill Splendens because of the opulence it embodied. Here Beckford luxuriated in wild Rococo extravagance surrounded by marble statuary, Persian rugs and vaulted passages draped with silk hangings. This palace of counter-Enlightenment exoticism was the scene, in 1781, of one of the country's most scandalous high society parties. At Christmas that year, Beckford hosted a decadent Bacchanal, employing the celebrated stage creator, Jacques Philippe de Loutherbourg, to turn Fonthill Splendens into a faery demon temple. The son et lumière spectacle of music and fireworks, of orgiastic feasting and love-making lasted several days but caused a scandal that endured considerably longer. But this was only one of the sexual scandals that eventually resulted in Beckford's expulsion from polite society.

After spending much of the next few years of his life abroad, Beckford returned to Fonthill Splendens. He concentrated his efforts on the creation of a landscape that would afford him privacy from a society that had deemed him sexually unacceptable. To screen his home from public view he planted a forbidding forest of spruce, larch and fir and surrounded the entire estate with a four-metre high wall known as the Barrier. Beckford's personal motto was 'secret and happy'. Today all that survives of Splendens is the Dark Walk and a grotto by Josiah Lane.

Beckford also commissioned the architect James Wyatt to build a gothic summer house in the grounds of Fonthill Splendens but the project grew out of hand and by 1807 Fonthill Abbey, the finest gothic revival building in England, had been built. Its tower soared to a height of nearly one hundred metres in a magnificent architectural gesture that was captured by painters such as Turner and inspired the writings of Byron. Fonthill fever swept the country, and spires and cloisters became the latest fashion accessory. Beckford left Fonthill Splendens and moved into the Abbey, whose vast baronial hall was entered through enormous doors, three storeys high. In a humorous contrast of scale the doorman was a malodorous Swiss dwarf in a gold suit, named Perro, whom Beckford had rescued from destitution in Geneva.

But Beckford, whose fortune had dwindled as the result of such extravagance, grew tired of his new creation and eventually sold Fonthill Abbey. On his deathbed the project's chief clerk confessed that he had not spent all the money on solid foundations for the building and, sure enough, on 21 December 1825, the towers came crashing down. The Abbey lay in ruins but a fragment of the north end still stands today, a monument to Beckford's obsessive whim.

In 1822 he moved to Bath, buying two adjacent houses. A bridge was built adjoining them, and a third house was later purchased to keep the neighbours at a

A sexual outcast from polite society, William Beckford built Lansdown Tower near Bath to indulge his need for privacy.

Each step of this spiral staircase in a building of debauched opulence was designed to elevate spatially and socially from the outside world.

discreet distance. The library was reached by means of a covered staircase that enabled Beckford, who had become eccentrically withdrawn, to ascend without being watched by passing servants. Lansdown Hill had also been acquired and a young architect, Henry Edmund Goodridge, was now engaged to build a tower on its summit.

Constructed of gilded cast iron and finely dressed blocks of locally quarried stone, the austerely Italianate edifice rose to a height of over fifty metres. The view from the top took in a total of six counties and it was to here that the recluse retreated each day. Luxuriously furnished rooms with names including the Sanctuary, and the Scarlet and Crimson Drawing Rooms, added an air of debauched opulence to the interior of a tower which now held the finest nineteenth-century collection of decorative arts in the country. Upward through its core wound a fabulous spiral staircase, each step designed to elevate its owner both spatially and socially from the world outside. From a lofty chamber known as the Belvedere it was possible to look through twelve windows that gave a superb view in every direction but from which almost nothing showed. The tower was crowned by a cupola and gilded lantern, a reproduction of Lysikrates' Choragic Monument that inspired the creators of numerous British follies.

That Beckford desired absolute privacy in his unconventional life was further emphasised by the garden that surrounded the tower. Although he stopped short of erecting a fortress-like wall as he had done at Fonthill Splendens, this wilderness of nature was designed to protect his isolation. There were no formal pathways, the only routes through being 'such as are worn by the passenger's feet', although a young Victoria managed to find her way through when she visited Lansdown Tower in 1830 before becoming Queen.

Beckford died in May of 1884 after getting soaked to the skin while out taking a walk. He wished to be buried in the grounds of the tower but the Bishop of Bath and Wells, doubtless aware of Beckford's reputation, refused to consecrate that ground so his body was interred at Lyncombe. Eventually, after Beckford's daughter purchased Lansdown Hill, the Bishop relented and the ground was consecrated. Beckford's body was disinterred and brought back to Lansdown where he now rests in a sarcophagus of his own design. It is probably only local legend that maintains that an oval ditch around his burial marks a small patch of land wickedly exempted from the Bishop's consecration.

Renaissance Britain had truly been a time of enlightenment and unrivalled sexual frankness. The creation of enormous family wealth had freed many individuals from the grind of daily work and characters such as Sir Francis Dashwood and William Beckford were sufficiently eccentric to do something memorable with their fortunes. It would be easy to condemn these hedonists, lechers and sodomites as frivolous spendthrifts but we should not forget that their libertine departures from the conventions of the day not only endowed the countryside with a sumptuous legacy of sexually inspired creations, but also started an undercurrent of cultural libertarianism that would set the tone for a more modern age.

The sensuous lines of the maze at Glendurgan gardens followed a tradition that was inspired by the naked female form.

CHAPTER EIGHT

We Are Surprisingly Amused

DOES IT NOT TAKE A MIND SOMEWHAT PREOCCUPIED WITH SEX TO
IMAGINE KNICKERS ON A PIANO?

E. JANE DICKINSON

What would come to most people's minds if asked to imagine typical Victorians? Morally upright parents in starched collars and whalebone corsets sitting with intimidated children in gloomy parlours where even the piano legs have been draped for decency? It all sounds familiar but let us suppose, for a moment, that this stereotype is wrong. The view of Victorians as sexually repressed was actually a later fabrication by early twentieth-century artists and writers. These forward-looking commentators of a new age required a conservative point of reference against which to measure their own modernity and liberalism – and that meant condemning their colourful predecessors to a reputation of dullness and prudery.

The nineteenth century was in fact an age of unparalleled adventure and invention, of high-velocity thrills and a surprising degree of permissiveness. The story about covering table legs with knickers to prevent indecent exposure was a myth. It arose from Frederick Marryat's accounts of travels in America and was repeated more in humour than in seriousness. Furthermore, any society that, even in jest, saw erotic symbolism in the sensuous curvature of a piano leg had to have sex already on the mind.

Sexuality was recognised, in the nineteenth century, as a central component of human existence.

With the power to shape – or undermine – the fabric of society, it was appropriate to subject the matter to reasoned consideration. It was these very attempts to describe and analyse sexuality that led to one of history's greatest discourses on the issue. New inventions stimulated the production of a massive body of erotic and pornographic material. Exciting new dioramas and kinematographs – which survive today in the form of the cinema – joined a growing body of printed material made widely available for the first time. With Mrs Beeton's style of helpfulness, 'practical information on sexual subjects could be found in standard household manuals, jostling with recipes for devilled kidneys and tips on how to repair cracked varnish'.

From the world of art the English Nude emerged, an elegantly proud – but definitely naked – creation. Lord Frederick Leighton's 'The Fisherman and the Syren' depicted that medieval symbol of watery seduction, the mermaid, described by one modern critic as an 'emblem of pure sex'. Audiences today are still entranced by 'Lilith', a work by John Collier in which a woman of undeniable charm is erotically entwined with a serpent – the ancient symbol of sexual appetite. The royal family were enthusiastic patrons of such works. The private chambers of Queen Victoria and Prince Albert were hung with explicit and erotic paintings bought for one another as birthday gifts.

So how was this unexpected degree of levity and sexual frankness reflected in the landscape? At the end of the eighteenth century, the landscape architect Erasmus Darwin had been expounding the appeal of laying out a garden in curves and circles inspired by the naked female form. Now, in a Rococo revival of the early 1800s, Sir Henry Stuart developed Darwin's ideas, planting trees and borders in sensuous ovals and wavy lines. A style that became known as 'gardenesque' or 'free symmetrical' swept Britain and was adopted by celebrated designers such as Humphry Repton and John Loudon. *Gardener's Magazine* began advocating the use of volutes, spirals and half-moons.

Encapsulated within the gardens of this time, it seems, were all the elements associated with ancient sexuality and fertility. Charles Fowler planted half-moon beds on the parterre at Syon Park; in the Swiss Garden at Old Warden in Bedfordshire a circular, mounded island rose from the lake, like Silbury Hill, from its symbolic primeval waters of creation. And at Glendurgan in Cornwall, Alfred Fox sculpted the most sensuous curves of all in his asymmetrical maze of cherry laurel, perpetuating that ancient symbol of female sexuality and scene of much amorous opportunity.

The Victorian era, though, most strongly evokes scenes of industrialisation and technological progress.

The upmarket Burlington Arcade in London, where both sex and shopping were pursued with equal vigour and transvestite youths were a speciality.

With the introduction of new machinery came an end, for many, of an ancient bond with the land. A tide of agricultural workers forced to leave their rural villages arrived in Britain's furiously expanding cities to supply the hungry factories with labour. At the beginning of the nineteenth century the population of London was around one hundred thousand. By 1901 there were eighteen cities in Britain of more than half a million people. And it was not just employment that was on offer in these mushrooming metropolises.

Brothels and fetish clubs became a highly visible element of entertainment in London, especially in the sex-focused culture of Soho. In the middle of the nineteenth century, the number of London women earning a living from prostitution was estimated at eighty thousand and mind-altering drugs were freely available over the counter of any pharmacy. Anyone walking down Old Compton or Wardour Streets today will see that the façades looking down from above street level are Victorian.

Within the fashionable and luxurious surroundings of the Burlington Arcade both sex and shopping were pursued with equal vigour. The Arcade, which lies off Piccadilly in the heart of London's West End, was commissioned by Lord George Cavendish in 1819. He lived next door in Burlington House and, so the story goes, built the Arcade to stop rowdy Londoners discarding oyster shells into his garden as they passed. The plan backfired, however, as Burlington Avenue soon gained a reputation for more than seafood. Men began frequenting the rooms above the bonnet shop where more was on sale than just hats. And despite the presence of uniformed beadles – veteran soldiers employed by Cavendish to maintain an air of decorum and respectability – available transvestite youths became a speciality of the up-market Burlington mall.

But by no means all assignations were lacking in romance. London's parks and pleasure gardens continued to provide fresh air and greenery – a much needed relief from the stony angularity of the polluted streets. And these were still places where chance encounters were possible. The site of Cremorne Gardens on the Chelsea Embankment near Battersea Bridge is now almost obscured by housing but a few bedding plants in brickwork containers on Cheyne Walk commemorate the name of what was one of the nineteenth century's liveliest 'cruising' grounds. An admission fee of one shilling opened up a wonderland of lights and music. Gas lanterns illuminated arbours where champagne was sipped and couples polka'd round an open-air dance floor to the sounds of an orchestra playing on a Chinoiserie bandstand. By 1862 it was possible to telegraph in advance to book a ringside seat by the crowded dance floor to hear music-hall entertainers make bawdy allusions to the sexual and narcotic pleasures of the park.

Few extensive public walks were established outside the capital but at the Belle Vue Gardens in Manchester, it was well known that proposition was as much the aim as perambulation. The park was extended from private grounds in 1833 and soon became an attraction of extravagant proportions. To an Italian Garden, hothouses and mazes were added the designs of Thomas Danson, including an Indian Mosque and rustic grottoes. And on occasion, extravagant spectacles such as the Siege of Khartoum and a Venetian Carnival were all part of the Belle Vue experience.

Alton Towers, Staffordshire: conservatories became the ultimate architectural accessory and indulged an insatiable Victorian appetite for the exotic.

Smaller towns, too, were not without their equivalent of the urban pleasure garden. Matlock Bath in Derbyshire, famous for the restorative powers of its thermal spas, was one the most popular Victorian destinations in Britain. The town was also the site of a walkway of rugged beauty and breath-taking views. The River Derwent here follows a turbulent course through a dark and precipitous gorge. Lined with lime trees and yew, a circular route still follows the ravine-bound river for some distance before steeply ascending a precipitous limestone cliff. It is ablaze in late spring with the blossoms of bluebells, cow parsley and celandines and from the giddy heights of the summit, the old spa town lies between the river and the rock. The exhilaration of this lofty route and the privacy found so far above the town no doubt lead to this path being known as Lovers' Walk.

As well as appreciating the joys of nature, Victorians were developing an insatiable appetite for increasingly novel spectacles with more than just a hint of the exotic. In answer to this clamour, Prince Albert masterminded the Great Exhibition at Crystal Palace in 1881. Its innovative glass construction – the first of its kind anywhere in the world – caused a sensation and hothouse fever swept the nation. Conservatories became the ultimate architectural accessory and no Victorian home was considered fashionable without that obligatory glass extension.

Even in the Outer Hebrides a curvilinear conservatory was added to Lews Castle in Stornoway. One critic scorned the addition of such an inappropriate structure, describing the glass house as 'hanging on to a baronial castle, like a Chinese Pagoda'. At Alton Towers in Staffordshire the glasshouse was an integral part of the gardens designed for the Earl of Shrewsbury by Thomas Allason and Robert Abrahams. But these delicate structures were not for the cultivation of ordinary indigenous species.

Sir Joseph Hooker, the son of the first director of Kew Gardens, made a series of expeditions to the Himalayan kingdom of Sikkim. Despite being illegally imprisoned for a time there, Hooker returned to Britain with twenty-eight species of outrageously coloured rhododendrons that caused a mania to match that begun by Crystal Palace. At Cragside in Northumberland several thousand of these heady exotic plants soon covered the grounds, 'blooming so profusely as to light up the whole hillside with their varied colours'. From all over the globe plant specimens were being brought for cultivation in British gardens and glass houses. Orchid houses were devoted solely to the nurturing of blooms whose fleshy tuberous roots earned it a Latin name, *Orkhis*, meaning testicles. The impact on the British landscape of such highly perfumed and richly coloured sense-arousing exotica would, in the words of one garden historian, have been 'the equivalent of introducing a harlot into the garden'.

Colour also became a wider contentious issue with some Victorians. At the International Exposition of 1862, John Gibson, one of the most celebrated sculptors of his day, caused a scandal with his display of the 'Tinted Venus'. Nudity in classical sculpture was considered publicly acceptable on the grounds of its monochrome appearance. White marble figurines embodied purity, virtue or courage; even Hiram Power's eroticised, sadomasochistic figure of a Greek slave was acceptable because of its monochromicity. Add a little colour, however   as Gibson daringly did to Venus's lips and nipples – and you have an immediate transformation from purity into flushed sites of unrestrained pleasure. Fuel was then added to the flames of argument by the claims of a new breed of professionals called archaeologists. The original statues from ancient Greece, it was revealed, were daubed in a multicoloured orgy of fleshy tones. The art world was in turmoil, divided between monochromists and those like the artist Lawrence Alma-Tadema who even painted his house to resemble the erotic frescoed walls of a classical Pompeiian villa.

One statue that met with widespread public approval was a winged figure of Eros, erected in

A statue of Eros threatens passers-by in London's Piccadilly Circus with an arrow from his bow.

213

London's Oxford Circus in 1893 as a memorial to Lord Shaftesbury. Eros was known as the product of Chaos and was instrumental in orchestrating the divine union between Uranus and Gaia – or Heaven and Earth. His poised, sleek outline still threatens shoppers and tourists in with an arrow from his gilded bow.

In the latter part of the century, a group of like-minded artists, architects and manufacturers began a reaction against established values that was to shake Victorian society to the core. The Arts and Crafts movement began as a desire to leave behind not only the ugliness of industrialisation but also the ostentation of imported exoticism. Exponents of the movement favoured a return to the romanticised rural idyll. Science had recently challenged the accepted doctrine of religion with paradigm-altering ideas on human evolution. Now the laws of nature were also turned to for artistic inspiration by artisans who sought not to dominate but to work in partnership with nature in a romanticised return to countrified ideals.

Traditional Victorian ideals were discarded and replaced with a vision drawn directly from Tennyson's Arthurian legends and the Pre-Raphaelite paintings of Dante Gabriel Rosetti and Edward Burne-Jones. Although medieval sources inspired this romantic and sexually charged nostalgia it was modern women, unsullied by industrialisation and commerce, who were perceived as the redeeming power. The artist and designer William Morris stood at the heart of this Bohemian group who embodied the new values of beauty, romance and nature. His beautiful wife Jane was portrayed by many contemporary artists as personifying a latent sexuality and element of savage nature that both fascinated and terrified the Victorian establishment. Such expressions of sexual desire, though otherwise taboo, were sanctified in the surreal context of the Pre-Raphaelites and the garden was considered fertile ground for this fantasy and illusion.

William Morris and Phillip Webb created a garden at Red House in Kent where the choice of flowers and shrubs was plucked directly from the Romantic verse that had stimulated this visual response. They blurred the division between the house interior and the outside garden by the creation of a sequence of semi-enclosed outdoor 'rooms'. Inspired by medieval gardens, these were highly scented with indigenous blossoms and provided a fitting backdrop to poetically amorous encounters.

A Hidden Garden, concealed behind a screen of yew and holly, with no obvious entrance and providing the ultimate setting for intimate or social encounters was also created by Gertrude Jekyll at her home in Surrey. Believing that a house and garden should appear to have grown up from the very rocks

At Kellie Castle in Fife, Lorimer encapsulated his views of love as a romanticised ideal in the creation of Cupid's Corner.

The Legend Gate at Earshall is inscribed with the words: 'He who loves his garden still keeps his Eden' and is topped with a fungoid phallus.

and soil around it, Munstead Wood comprised an exquisitely simple design using traditional techniques and local craftsmen and materials. While classical architecture exerted the idea of human domination over nature, Romantic architecture took nature as its inspiration. The ideal had 'the vitality and profusion of something of the soil; the rhythms majestic or tender of the earth; in colour and structure sublimates sensuous faculties. Its effect is to voice the poetry of nature, the wonder in human life. It is emotional, sensuous, cumulative.'

At New Place in Haslemere, Surrey, the architect Charles Voysey designed a garden for the publisher Sir Algernon Methuen in 1897. With the intention of ennobling the thoughts and feelings of his clients, Voysey repeatedly employed the heart motif as a reference to noble and romantic love. Heart shapes were worked into woodcarvings, letterboxes and chair-backs. He designed a sunken garden in which the centre piece was a heart-shaped flower bed filled with rue although Lady Methuen, it seems, objected on the grounds that it was 'hardly practical . . . and I do not care for the scent'. Gertrude Jekyll was asked to re-design the garden five years later.

Vita Sackville-West was among the members of high society who visited the gardens at Hidcote inspired by the Arts and Crafts movement. Deep in the Cotswolds their American owner, Lawrence Waterburg Johnston, manipulated the quintessential elements of the English country garden with the objectivity of a foreigner – much to Ms West's delight. She wrote: 'I had become so wildly intoxicated by the spilling abundance of Hidcote that I was no longer in any mood to worry about exact nomenclature, but only in the mood to enjoy the next pleasure to be presented.'

This bud of new Romanticism was also starting to blossom further north, across the Scottish border. Rising from fertile arable land that slopes gently to the south and the waters of the Firth of Forth just west of Anstruther in Fife is Kellie Castle. Since the fifteenth century the onshore breeze has stirred leaves around this fortified house. Its walls are not the grey, forbidding architecture of many grand Scottish houses but a dusky sandstone pink that catches the summer evening light on an intriguing collection of turrets, castellations and round-angle towers.

Kellie Castle was renovated by Professor James Lorimer, who took up residence there in 1878. When he was not practising law in Edinburgh, Lorimer toiled outdoors to turn a gnarled and neglected plot into one of Scotland's finest gardens. The word most often used to describe Kellie is 'romantic' and it is not difficult to imagine why. An unassuming doorway in the south side of a high garden wall leads from the

salt-tinged air of open fields into an unexpected walled paradise. In high summer, the flowerbeds overflow with heavy-headed indigenous blooms that thrive in this sheltered corner of the estate. Songbirds trilling amongst branches in the garden compete with the cawing of crows lodged high in woodland trees beyond – an acoustic demonstration of the Arts and Crafts belief that nurtured beds should gradually give way to wilderness.

Lorimer divided the walled garden into quadrants. The south-east corner, known as the Secret Garden or Cupid's Corner, was enclosed by a dense yew hedge. On a central pedestal he erected a statue of Cupid which seemed to encapsulate his views of love as a romanticised ideal. An accomplished lawyer, Lorimer was also a talented amateur painter. 'A Homage to Cupid' hangs in the Drawing Room of Kellie Castle and features a pagan scene of willowy maidens worshipping around the elevated figurine. The artist Phoebe Traquair was also inspired by this mystical corner of the garden but painted her Cupid mural on the Drawing Room wall.

It was in this scented sylvan world that his son grew up. Robert Lorimer would become one of Scotland's most celebrated architects and landscape designers – and fervent subscriber to Arts and Crafts ideals. He sought 'that beauty which mankind, with simplicity of heart and infinite pains, may capture

Carved stone monkeys, a medieval symbol of lust, play along the Tool House roof.

The doors of the Dowry House or Apple Store have been carved with hearts.

from nature and reproduce in his works'. His devotion to this work was serious but Robert also displayed a light-hearted side inherited, perhaps, from his father. He advocated the creation of gardens in which stood a single woodland deity, half-smothered in honeysuckle or wild rose: 'just one Pan, ready to twitch the Nymph's last garment off'.

Upon completing his apprenticeship with an architectural firm in London, Robert Lorimer's first commission, in 1892, was at the magnificent sixteenth-century tower house of Earlshall. Between the Scottish towns of Dundee and St Andrews, the round towers and turrets of Earlshall are still the image of a fairytale castle. And here, within the architectural details that lie hidden within the grounds, Lorimer freely expressed his passion for the romantic ideal.

Although the grounds have recently been the subject of a careful programme of restoration a delightful air of 'secret garden' adds an almost tangible scent of intrigue to the castle surroundings. As at Kellie Castle, the garden is entirely enclosed by a high stone wall. To step inside is like entering Lewis Carroll's surreal Wonderland of gigantic topiary chess pieces. Perhaps the reference to this contemporary work was a deliberate one since there are other equally abstract and sexually symbolic features to be discovered. The wall is breached at several points by

overgrown doorways that demand further exploration.

The Legend Gate leads from the garden to a woodland beyond that is filled with birdsong and carpeted with lush and pungent foliage. On the woodland side, beneath two engraved hearts, is the inscription: 'He who loves his garden still keeps his Eden.' If this was an erotic reference to the garden where woman first tempted man, then it is graphically emphasised by the inclusion of a fungoid phallus atop the gateway pediment.

Back inside the walled garden, a short walk past rows of trained fruit trees ends, in one corner, at the Tool House. This marvellous old stone structure still houses piles of plant pots and smells of dusty earth. Along the roof slates scamper five carved stone monkeys. These creatures were a medieval symbol of the vice of lust and their sensual appearance is emphasised by one of the monkeys gorging on a succulent piece of fruit. But the Tool House is no Romanesque church so we must suspect that their role here is humorous – perhaps even encouraging what the medieval clergy sought to forbid.

More equally mischievous monkeys can be seen adorning the gable end of Lorimer's Dowry House. They hang above the window of this romantic retreat tucked away in the north-west corner of the garden. This quaint edifice also used to be known as the Apple

Store and the monkeys perch either side of a crest that bears the emblem of an apple. An outside staircase leads up one wall to a rustic first-floor doorway above which is carved a whole basket full of apples. The significance of the apple in Lorimer's Eden, especially when accompanied by hosts of lustful monkeys, would not have been lost on an educated Victorian audience.

Beneath this gable window is a pair of wooden doors that are carved in a similar fashion to what one imagines Voysey's abundant hearts at New Place to have been. Both gardens were created at around the same time so it is not unlikely that the imagery in play at New Place – designed to invoke notions in the onlooker of ideal love – was also intended at Earlshall. But glancing up once more, our gaze is met once more by the pair of libidinous, yet undeniably appealing, creatures, so what was Lorimer's message here? Perhaps that, in the confines of a secret garden, it was acceptable to temper noble love with a little 'monkey business'?

These covert glimpses, it seems, hint at a surprisingly colourful Victorian society. An outwardly proper appearance was the fashionable veneer of the time but beneath society's composed exterior pulsed a desire for adventure, romance and the exotic. All these variously found expression in the Victorian landscape from the brothels of Soho to the genteel gardens of Fife. Although the established view of Victorians as universally prudish has had to be re-evalued in recent years, it cannot be denied that this was a complex society and that a puritan element found difficulty in resolving some issues relating to public sexuality. Many of the medieval exhibitionist church sculptures were removed or destroyed in the nineteenth century by those who misunderstood their iconography. But, as Salvador Dali wrote, however: 'Revulsion is the sentinel at the door to our deepest desires.'

It seems regrettable that the person who embodied the era is remembered for a quote she never said. Queen Victoria, to the contrary it seems, was often very amused. Thankfully, enough Victorian landscapes and built environments have survived the intervening decades to allow us to re-evaluate our closest ancestors. So many of our own values and customs are deeply rooted in those of the nineteenth century it would be to do ourselves an injustice if we did not credit the Victorians with an element of capricious sexuality. They were represented, after all, by a monarch who possessed one of Britain's most impressive collections of erotic art.

Monkeys holding an apple crest symbolise the sexual temptation Man in the Garden of Eden.

219

The Biomes house the steamy, scented world of the Eden Project.

CHAPTER NINE

Sign of the Times

PYLONS, THOSE PILLARS
BARE LIKE NUDE, GIANT GIRLS THAT HAVE NO SECRET.

STEPHEN SPENDER

Sexual symbolism is perhaps more prevalent today than at any other time in history. Our modern, predominantly urban, surroundings are crowded with explicit images, many of which transpose a desire to copulate into a desire to consume. Sex, after all, does sell. But although the theme is nothing new, these images are transient and fleeting – today's billboard cleavage will be a four-wheel drive tomorrow. We do not have to go very far, though, to find places where memories are a little longer.

The number of visitors to ancient sites is growing year on year – and people don't just come to picnic. Sites such as Castlerigg in the English Lake District still command our attention nearly five thousand years after the first stones were erected. Every year a vast crowd assembles at Stonehenge to witness for themselves the spectacle of sunrise at midsummer. So what is it that still draws us to these places in the twenty-first century?

Stone circles, Roman temples, even stately gardens, offer a connection to the landscape that, for many of us, has been lost. In the past the enduring link between people and the landscape was openly acknowledged – a subtle relationship in which health and abundance were both recognised and hoped for. But if, as humans, we still feel a connection to our environment, why are we not building circles of our own – erecting concrete pillars and steel monuments to sexuality in a modern age?

One of the fundamental changes in recent history has been diminishing access to the land. Britain and Ireland in 3000 BC were sparsely populated and vast areas of virgin territory lay untouched – a natural

'The Rites of Dionysus': naked figures writhe and dance in savage and intoxicated revelry.

canvas waiting to be painted. The first farmers began an irreversible process of dividing and fencing-off the land into privately owned plots. More recently, since the Industrial Revolution, swathes of remaining countryside have disappeared under layers of concrete or cash crops. Not fertile ground for creative expression. But although, for most of us, monumental works on the scale of Castlerigg are no longer a possibility, we are now presented with different stimuli. Like Stephen Spender's naked pylons, today's surroundings still inspire an interpretation of our environment as deeply sexual. And, within the apparent constraints of a planning-regulated landscape, new opportunities are evolving for the expression of sexuality and desire.

From the depths of a former china clay pit near St Austell in Cornwall, gigantic spheres have risen like glistening larvae. Inside the hexagonal facets of these geodesic domes, global environments are incubated on a manageable scale. What was once an infertile, post-industrial wasteland now houses tropical and temperate flora in the steamy, scented world of the Eden Project. The story of the symbiotic relationship between humans and plants told here has proved to be an absorbing one, but amid the twisting roots and concealing leaves can also be found some of Britain's most powerful – and surprisingly erotic – art.

Where coiling tendrils of grape vines probe the red Mediterranean earth, Dionysus – Greek god of vines, intoxication and savage revelry – rises as a mighty, virile bull. Among the vines that were the source of intoxication and symbol of immortality, naked figures writhe and dance. These are the Maenads – the mythological followers of Dionysus. Their orgiastic worship of the vines induces a heady concoction of violence and ecstasy, portrayed at Eden through the sexual, primeval energy of the forms. 'The Rites of Dionysus' is the work of Cornish-based sculptor Tim Shaw and, although contemporary in its approach, this public sculpture is inspired by the legends of a culture more than two thousand years old. Less directly, it seems, ancient elements have also influenced the work of another artist – this time in an altogether more private setting.

Dungeness on the Kent shore is a landscape of haunting surrealism. One of the largest shingle beds in the world, this place feels exposed, almost fragile, in the dominating presence of a nuclear reactor. Everything here is bleached by intense sunlight, burnt by salt-laden winds and struggling for a foothold among the soil-starved pebbles yet at Dungeness, Derek Jarman created a unique garden of moving and simple beauty.

The artist, film maker and gay rights activist moved to Prospect Cottage after learning he was HIV

The timber pillars and iron rings bring their earthy connotations of human sexuality to this shingle garden.

positive. Jarman began to create a therapeutic and changing art form in the stones around his home using driftwood and debris collected from the beach. Rusted metal spikes, coils and sea-washed wooden posts were hauled back to the garden where they were placed in a series of abstract arrangements. Although recently erected, the timber pillars seem to stand with an air of permanence and Jarman, in fact, cited prehistoric dolmens as his inspiration. The influence of stone circles can be seen, too, in the round pebble formations and raked concentric gravel rings, bringing to the shingle their earthy connotations of human sexuality. Many of the shapes here seem to be deliberately penetrative: holed stones threaded onto

Many of the shapes in Derek Jarman's garden are overtly penetrative.

wooden sticks, iron pillars piercing rings of pebbles or cork. The whole garden is a work of tender attention to detail and yet it aches with anger, too.

Among the narrow streets of old St Ives, halfway up a steep cobbled hill and hidden behind a high wall, is hidden another, much lusher, retreat. Here, in Cornwall's subtropical climate, exotic lilies and palms blend gracefully with the more English varieties of roses and a copper beech in the grounds of Trewyn Studio, home to one of the twentieth century's most fascinating sculptors.

Barbara Hepworth exhibited many of the larger pieces she created in a garden that was for her own pleasure rather than for public display. Their strong verticals and sensuously smooth curves seem at ease in this natural setting; indeed, many of them were inspired by nature itself. Through sculpture, Hepworth explored the relationship between people and their surroundings – a bond she saw as 'the very essence of life'. She was drawn to the pagan landscape around St Ives and the influence of standing stones and sites such as Men-an-Tol upon her work is unmistakable. She sought an abstract beauty in the soaring pillars and round, pierced forms that arose directly from that landscape.

Another outdoor space inspired by shapes formerly associated with fertility has been created in the grounds of a Victorian villa in rural Oxfordshire. Between the elegant red brick house and swathes of surrounding corn field, a mature garden unrolls like a luxurious carpet. Textures range from a velvet lawn, the lacy fronds of larch and the sculpted spikes of monkey puzzle trees but everywhere are shades of green – from brilliant lime to nearly black. Exploring hidden corners of the garden reveals numerous carefully laid out motifs. Although formed in different types of stone, these are all variations on a spiral design and at the centre of the garden lies the most ambitious of them all.

A dense hedge conceals a circular pattern in the grass over twenty metres in diameter. What appears, at first glance, to be broad concentric circles is

Ancient symbols of human sexuality endure in the circles and vertical lines of Barbara Hepworth's sculpture.

Prehistoric sites such as Men-an-Tol provided inspiration for the artist's work.

actually a winding spiral path. Its complex and convoluted course, reminiscent of early labyrinths, is marked in pale paving stones and eventually loops from a point on the perimeter all the way to the centre of the maze. The labyrinth is the work of photographer John Comino-James and it was designed to be paced. There is surely nowhere more conducive to quiet reflection than a garden such as this and if contemplation is the aim of following the labyrinth's mesmerising curves then it is poignant that its form echoes ancient designs that once represented the cyclical nature of life and rebirth.

In contrast, at Wallington Hall in Northumberland a very light hearted approach has been taken to the modern landscape. In the eighteenth century, Sir Walter Calverley Blackett turned eighty acres of bleak fells into a romantic pleasure ground of parkland and follies. Over two hundred years later, in the autumn of 2001, artists, dancers, musicians and designers came together to recreate some of Wallington's original eccentricity. Their brief was to interpret the theme of unrequited love through a series of follies created in situ among the sycamores and bluebells of the East Wood. So, while the fashion over two hundred years ago was for gardens to err on the side of the licentious, these modern pieces had to illustrate unconsummated longing in what has truly become a landscape of desire.

The spiralling lines of this private modern maze echo ancient designs that once represented the cyclical nature of life and regeneration.

227

'The Flower Bed': 'Love looks not with the eyes, but with the mind; And therefore is winged Cupid painted blind' – *A Midsummer Night's Dream*.

'The Flower Bed' is the work of local artists John Codd and Philippa Hodkinson. A bed seems at first a rather incongruous item to encounter within a woodland, but its frame of rough-hewn logs and linen of soft grass interspersed with delicate pink and white flowers – blends invitingly into these leafy surroundings. The double pillows and tousled sheets bring associations or expectations of love-making, especially when overlooked by a cupid-like cherub. But there is no passion here and the flowers will wither and die leaving only a hard, unmade structure of wood and shale.

A similar tale is portrayed in Malcolm Webster's 'Fountain of the Jilted Lover'. A sports car – that classically romantic image of the twentieth century – forms the focus of a scene in which the bride, initially enticed by such material trappings, has second thoughts, leaving the marriage unconsummated – and the groom to drown his sorrows in the lake. These and other sculptures formed the setting for performances the following summer reminiscent of Dashwood's eighteenth-century dedication of the Temple of Bacchus. Processions with costumes and music led audiences around the lake and lantern-lit gardens in a modern outdoor celebration of human life and love.

Fifty miles further east, on a late November day in 2000, a gigantic structure cruised slowly up the River Tyne. The Millennium Bridge was the first new construction to span the river in over one hundred years. Its design was unique but the sweeping double arc soon formed a sympathetic component of one of the north of England's most famous views. The bridge also linked the city of Newcastle to a newly developed cultural area on the South Bank. Renovations included the transformation of a 1950s flour warehouse into Europe's biggest art factory and exhibition space – the Baltic. Julian Opie was commissioned to create artwork that would adorn this ambitious new area and what he unveiled has certainly re-written the rules on urban design.

Sprawled across a glass cubicle on the South Bank is the outline of a very relaxed – and very naked – male figure. A similarly disrobed female nude reposes on the north side of the river. Their simple silhouettes in black vinyl are echoed on the upper floor of the Baltic where an elevated couple are lovingly entwined. This is art in the most public sense and Opie's figures effortlessly encapsulate the very modern concepts of sex and the city.

Another, less blatant, reclining figure lies concealed at the heart of a story of a landscape's regeneration and rebirth. From the sixteenth century, Heligan House near the Cornish fishing village of Mevagissey was the seat of the Tremayne family. Exotic gardens were cultivated in the subtropical climate here including an Italianate garden inspired by

At Wallington Hall's 'Fountain of the Jilted Lover', the sorrows of an unconsummated marriage are drowned in the lake.

Sprawled across a glass cubicle on the south bank of the Millennium Bridge is the stark outline of a very relaxed – and very naked – male figure.

discoveries at Pompeii, romantic grottoes, and a tropical valley of palms and bamboo in which, according to rumour, half the population of Mevagissey were conceived. But following the First World War, the gardens were neglected. Overgrown with ivy, laurel and brambles they were not

rediscovered until many years later when Tim Smit and John Willis came upon the tangled ruins.

The lost gardens of Heligan have now been restored to their former verdant glory. As part of the garden's re-creation, local artists Sue and Peter Hill added 'Mudmaid' to the heady exoticism of tropical

'The Mudmaid' is an organic expression of sensuality and desire.

plants and the wild lure of native Cornish woodland. The sumptuous curves of this reclining female, while mirrored in the lushness of the vegetation from which she is formed, also seem to be melting into the earth. Her organic body is returning to the ground that first inspired such expressions of sensuality and desire.

Although the 'Mudmaid' portrays a serendipitous end to a journey through five thousand years of expression and interpretation of sexuality outdoors, her leaves and flowers will reappear in spring as part of the intimate and ongoing story of sex and the landscape.

Their Rituals provided the description of the club's aim. The remarks on the 'shameless' behaviour of the Beggar's Benison group come from an article in the *Guardian* (January 19 2002). General remarks about the pleasure gardens of London are taken from *A History of Courting* by E.S. Turner (p. 88) including the references to Tom Brown's 'Amusements Serious and Comical' and the words of Sir Roger de Coverley. The anonymous account of Vauxhall Park written in 1801 is reproduced in John Kelly's web article 'Parks and Pleasure Gardens of Regency London'. Comments on the frequent visitors to St James's Park are also from this article. The descriptions of Sir Francis Delaval and Seaton Delaval Hall are taken from *Those Delavals* by Roger Burgess. William Beckford's dislike of contemporary popular culture is discussed in an article in the *Guardian* (February 9 2002) by Sarah Wise entitled 'The man who had too much'.

Chapter Eight
WE ARE SURPRISINGLY AMUSED

The opening quotation is taken from an article in the *Radio Times* entitled 'Unlacing the Victorian Corset' by E. Jane Dickson, (20–26 January 2001) p. 19. The remarks on household manuals can be found in Matthew Sweet's *Inventing the Victorians* (p. 212). The critic discussing Victorian art is John Walsh writing for the *Independent* on 20 October 2001. References to Lews Castle, Stornoway and Cragside in Northumberland come from *Victorian Gardens* by Brent Elliot, pages 67 and 195 respectively. The garden historian quoted is Chris Beardshaw from the BBC's Flying Gardener programme (Series 2) in reference to the gardens at Knightshayes Court near Tiverton in Devon. The reference to the sensuous ideals of the Arts and Crafts movement comes from *The Work of Sir Robert Lorimer* by Christopher Hussey (p. 1). Quotations from Lady Methuen and Vita Sackville West are taken from *Arts and Crafts Gardens* by Wendy Hitchmough. 'Just one Pan' is quoted from Hussey's *The Work of Sir Robert Lorimer* (p. 22).

Chapter Nine
SIGN OF THE TIMES

Stephen Spender's lines from 'The Pylons' are from *Collected Poems 1928–1985*, p. 39. The quotation from Barbara Hepworth is taken from the Tate publication *Barbara Hepworth 1999* by Matthew Gale and Chris Stephens.

Further Reading

Chapter One

Timothy Darvill, Katherine Barker and Barbara Bender, *The Cerne Giant: An Antiquity on Trial*, Oxford: Oxbow, 1999

Ron Scholes, *Understanding the Countryside*, Waltham Abbey: Fraser Stewart, 1985

Chapter Two

John Barnatt, *Prehistoric Cornwall: The Ceremonial Monuments*, Wellingborough: Turnstone Press, 1982

Aubrey Burl, *A Guide to the Stone Circles of Britain, Ireland and Brittany*, Yale University Press, 1995

———, *Rites of the Gods*, JM Dent, 1981

———, *Prehistoric Avebury*, Yale University Press, 1979

Julian Cope, *The Modern Antiquarian*, Thorsons, 1998

Michael Dames, *The Avebury Cycle*, Thames and Hudson, 1977

Christopher Morris (ed.), *The Illustrated Journeys of Celia Fiennes 1685–c1712*, MacDonald & Co., 1982

Timothy Taylor, *The Prehistory of Sex: Four Million Years of Human Sexual Culture*, Fourth Estate, 1996

Chapter Three

Martyn Barber, David Field and Peter Topping, *The Neolithic Flint Mines of England*, Swindon: English Heritage and The Royal Commission on the Historical Monuments of England, 1999

Richard Bradley, *The Significance of Monuments*, Routledge, 1998

Alex Gibson and Derek Simpson (eds), *Prehistoric Ritual and Religion*, Stroud: Sutton, 1998

Ian McNeil Cooke, *Mother and Sun: The Cornish Fogou*, Penzance: Men-an-Tol Studio Publications, 1998

Ann Woodward, *British Barrows: A Matter of Life and Death*, Stroud: Tempus 2000

Chapter Four

Stan Beckinsall, *Northumberland's Prehistoric Rock Carvings*, Rothbury: Pendulum Publications, 1983

Janet Bord, *Sacred Waters: Holy Wells and Water Lore of Britain and Ireland*, Granada, 1985

Richard Bradley, *Rock Art and the Prehistory of Atlantic Europe*, Routledge 1997

Peter Cherici, *Celtic Sexuality: Power, Paradigm and Passion*, Duckworth, 1995

Evan Hadingham, *Ancient Carvings in Britain: A Mystery*, The Garnstone Press, 1974

Chapter Five

David Breeze and Brian Dobson, *Hadrian's Wall*, 4th edn, Penguin Books, 2000

John Clarke, *Looking at Lovemaking: Constructions of Sexuality in Roman Art, 100BC–AD250*, California University Press, 1998

Martin Millet, *Roman Britain*, English Heritage, 1995

Reay Tannahill, *Sex in History*, Hamish Hamilton, 1980

Chapter Six

Janet and Colin Bord, *Earth Rites: Fertility Practices in Pre Industrial Britain*, Book Club Associates, 1982

John Harvey, *Medieval Gardens*, Batsford, 1981

Conan Kennedy, *Ancient Ireland – The User's Guide*, Killah: Morrigan Books, 1994

Charles Thomas, *Tintagel: Arthur and Archaeology*, Batsford/ English Heritage, 1993

Anthony Weir and James Jerman, *Images of Lust: Sexual Carvings on Medieval Churches*, Routledge, 1993

Jennifer Westwood, *Albion: A Guide to Legendary Britain*, Granada, 1985

Chapter Seven

Jane Brown, *The Pusuit of Paradise: A Social History of Gardens and Gardening*, Harper Collins, 1999

Sir Francis Dashwood, *The Dashwoods of West Wycombe*, Aurum Press 1987

David Jacques, *Georgian Gardens: The Reign of Nature*, Batsford, 1983

Barbara Jones, *Follies and Grottoes*, Constable & Co., 1953

Susan Lasdun, *The English Park: Royal, Private and Public*, Andrew Deutsch, 1991

James Lees-Milne, *William Beckford*, Century, 1990

David Stevenson, *The Beggar's Benison: Sex Clubs of Enlightenment Scotland and Their Rituals*, Tuckwell Press, 2002

Chapter Eight

Clifford Bishop and Xenia Osthelder (eds), *Sexualia: From Prehistory to Cyberspace*, Cologne: Konemann, 2001

Brent Elliot, *Victorian Gardens*, Batsford, 1986

Wendy Hitchmough, *Arts and Crafts Gardens*, Pavilion, 2000

Roger Phillips and Nicky Foy, *A Photographic Garden History*, Macmillan, 1995

Matthew Sweet, *Inventing the Victorians*, Faber and Faber, 2001

Chapter Nine

Matthew Gale and Chris Stephens, *Barbara Hepworth*, Tate, 2001

Derek Jarman, *Derek Jarman's Garden*, with photographs by Howard Sooley, Thames and Hudson, 1995

Tim Smit, *The Lost Gardens of Heligan*, Orion 1999

Site Gazetteer

This gazetteer is designed be helpful to anyone wishing to visit the sites described in *Landscapes and Desire* for themselves.

It is arranged in a broad regional format, under which site names appear in alphabetical order. The site name (as it appears in the book) is followed by a monument type. The county or region is given next followed by a 6-figure National Grid reference and 1:50,000 scale Ordnance Survey Landranger sheet. These are correct to the best of our knowledge but please navigate with sense and caution. Grid references are not given for London sites as a location with reference to streets or landmarks was deemed to be more helpful, or for the Channel Islands, which lie outside the British Ordnance Survey scheme.

We have tried to note whenever sites are in the care of a national body, such as Historic Scotland or National Trust. Sites that lie within private land but which can be visited with the landowner's permission are included in the gazetteer. For those on or near public footpaths access is usually permitted by custom but if there is any doubt, permission should be sought at the nearest residence. The use of an up-to-date Ordnance Survey map (such as the Landranger series quoted) is strongly recommended especially when seeking to visit remoter places.

Many of the sites within this book are ancient or unique, potentially fragile and often within farmland or areas of incredible natural beauty. A gentle presence at these sites will ensure that this erotic legacy remains intact and accessible for future generations to enjoy.

ENGLAND

CENTRAL

Alkborough Maze (p. 163), Humberside
SE 880 218, Landranger Sheet 106
Signposted as Julian's Bower.

Alton Towers (p. 212), gardens, Staffordshire
SK 075 434, Landranger Sheet 119
These gardens share the site of a well signposted adventure park.

Bolsover Castle (p. 167), Derbyshire
SK 470 706 Landranger Sheet 120
The castle, 5 miles east of Chesterfield, is in the care of English Heritage.

Castle Howard (p. 189), Yorkshire
SE 716 700, Landranger Sheet 100
Stately home and landscaped gardens near York, still in the care of the Howard family but open to the public.

Kilpeck (p. 145), exhibitionist carving, Herefordshire
SO 444 304, Landranger Sheet 149

Lovers' Walk (p. 212), Derbyshire
SK 295 585, Landranger Sheet 119
A route follows level ground beside the river and scales the towering cliffs behind. Reached by a narrow footbridge over the river from the main road through Matlock Bath.

Bolsover Castle.

Mam Tor (p. 86), hill, Derbyshire
SK 128 837, Landranger Sheet 110
Mam Tor lies within the Peak District National Park. There are numerous navigable routes to its summit but use of an Ordnance Survey map is recommended.

Stowe (p. 172), landscape park, Buckinghamshire
SP 680 375, Landranger Sheet 152
The house and gardens at Stowe are in the care of the National Trust and are well signposted.

LONDON
Burlington Arcade (p. 210)
Off Burlington Gardens near the Royal Academy, just west of Piccadilly Circus.

Eros Statue (p. 213)
Piccadilly Circus at the junction of Regent Street and Piccadilly.

Ranelagh Park (p. 195)
On the north bank of the River Thames near Chelsea Bridge.

St James's Park (p. 197)
Near Buckingham Palace and Whitehall on the north bank of the River Thames, a quarter of a mile from Westminster Bridge.

Vauxhall Park (p. 197)
On the south side of the River Thames, a quarter of a mile south-east of Vauxhall Bridge.

NORTH
Birdoswald, Roman fort, and phalluses on **Hadrian's Wall** (p. 123)
NZ 615 663 and NZ 617 664, Cumbria Landranger Sheet 86
This fort is curated by the National Trust and English Heritage.

The two phalluses carved on the Roman Wall nearby are reachable by public footpath 23.5 metres and 206 metres respectively along the wall to the east, both carved on the southern face. This site is on the Hadrian's Wall National Path.

Bride's Chair (p. 157), natural stone seat, Lancashire
SD 483 730, Landranger Sheet 97
This natural feature lies at the foot of Warton Crags.

Castlerigg (p. 25), stone circle, Cumbria
NY 292 237, Landranger Sheet 90
The stone circle lies in a field just over 1 mile to the east of Keswick; it has open access and is cared for by the National Trust.

Chesters (p. 116), Roman fort, Northumberland
NY 912 702, Landranger Sheet 87
Curated by English Heritage and signposted. This site is on the route of the Hadrian's Wall National Path.

Chollerford (p. 122, Roman bridge, Northumberland
NY 914 701, Landranger Sheet 87
The bridge is accessible free of charge by footpath from the east side of the river North Tyne.

Coventina's Well (p. 112), sacred spring, Northumberland
NY 858 711, Landranger Sheet 87
The spring is situated in a shallow depression near the Mithraic Temple. The Hadrian's Wall National Path passes this site.

The Hermitage (p. 160, Northumberland
NU 242 060, Landranger Sheet 81
A pathway behind Warkworth Castle leads along the River Coquet to a point opposite this rock-cut structure. The Hermitage can then be reached by crossing the river by boat provided by English Heritage during the spring and summer months.

Castlerigg stone circle.

Housesteads (p. 113), Roman fort, Northumberland
NY 790 688, Landranger Sheet 86
Curated by English Heritage and well signposted. This site is on the route of the Hadrian's Wall National Path.

Little Meg (p. 107), carved stone circle, Cumbria
NY 577 375, Landranger Sheet 91
This tiny circle with its spiral carved stone lies at the edge of a field just half a mile to the east of the larger site of Long Meg. It is not signposted but worth navigating to find.

Long Meg and her Daughters (p. 34), stone circle, Cumbria
NY 571 372, Landranger Sheet 91
Six miles north-east of Penrith between the villages of Little Salkeld and Melmerby. Long Meg lies in an area of farmed land but there is no restriction of access to the stones.

Middleton (p. 126), Roman milestone, Cumbria
SD 623 858, Landranger Sheet 97
The stone is visible on an area of raised ground overlooking the valley of the River Lune.

Millennium Bridge (p. 228), Tyne and Wear
NZ 255 640, Landranger Sheet 88
Accessible by foot from north and south quaysides.

Petting Stone (p. 157), Lindisfarne Island, Northumberland
NU 126 418, Landranger Sheet 75
The stone can be found in the churchyard of Lindisfarne Priory, reachable via a causeway only at low tide. The Priory is in the care of English Heritage.

Prior Leschman's Chantry (p. 152), Northumberland
NY 935 642, Landranger Sheet 87
Located within Hexham Abbey.

Seaton Delaval Hall and **Starlight Castle** (p. 198), folly, Northumberland
NZ 322 766 and NZ 333 762, Landranger Sheet 88
Partly ruinous house 5 miles north of Tynemouth, signposted and still in the care of the Delaval family.

Sedbergh (p. 101), track and waterfall, Cumbria
SD 681 975, Pathfinder map 617, Landranger Sheet 98.
Although the trackway is not visible, a modern footpath leads to Cautley Spout waterfall from the south-east following Courtley Holme Beck.

Vindolanda (p. 122), Roman fort, Northumberland
NY 771 664, Landranger Sheet 86
The site of Vindolanda is in private ownership but open to visitors.

Wallington Hall (p. 227), house and gardens, Northumberland
NZ 028 843, Landranger Sheet 81
Wallington Hall lies just south of the village of Cambo and is cared for by the National Trust.

Weetwood Moor (p. 105), prehistoric art site, Northumberland
NU 022 282, Landranger Sheet 75
A complex of carved stones lies just to the north of a path that leads across the moor from near a cattle grid on the track. Site requires the use of an Ordnance Survey map.

Yeavering Bell (p. 89), Iron Age twin-peaked hill fort, Northumberland
Centred NT 928 293, Landranger Sheet 75
Yeavering Bell can be reached either by a steep climb from the north or a gentler approach across moorland from the south.

Vindolanda Roman fort.

SOUTH-EAST

Buckland (p. 147), exhibitionist carving, Buckinghamshire
SP 888 125, Landranger Sheet 165
The carving can be found on the first wall of All Saints' Church to be seen upon entering the churchyard (south side) directly above the wooden Priests' Door.

Canterbury Medieval Carving (p. 152)
TR 150 580 Landranger Sheet 179
Under a first-floor overhang on Palace Street.

Fishbourne (p. 129), Roman palace, Sussex
SU 830 050, Landranger Sheet 197
Extensive Roman villa including a mosaic of Cupid riding on a dolphin. The site, 2 miles west of Chichester, is run by the Sussex Archaeological Society and is open to the public.

Grimes Graves (p. 71), Neolithic flint mines, Norfolk
TL 817 900, Landranger Sheet 144
Five miles north-west of Thetford, the site is curated by English Heritage and one of the shafts can be descended into by ladder.

Hever Castle (p. 165), Kent
TQ 478 452, Landranger Sheet 188

Hilton (p. 165), medieval village maze
TL 293 663, Landranger Sheet 153
Hilton village lies 10 miles north-west of Cambridge. The maze can be found on the village green.

Ickwell (p. 155), maypole, Bedfordshire
TL 149 455, Landranger Sheet 153
The maypole stands in one corner of the extensive village green at Ickwell in Bedfordshire and is accessible to the public. Annual May Day celebrations still take place.

Derek Jarman's Garden (p. 223), Kent
TR 095 170, Landranger Sheet 189
Prospect Cottage, Dungeness. This is now a private residence and visitors are requested to be respectful of the owner's privacy.

Long Man of Wilmington (p. 9), Sussex
TQ 543 035 Landranger Sheet 199
Chalk figure on north-facing slopes of Windover Hill, visible from the ground.

Medmenham Abbey (p. 179), Buckinghamshire
SU 807 838, Landranger Sheet 175
Medmenham Abbey is now a private residence and is not open to visitors. A public footpath along the south side of the Thames does, however, provide an excellent view over the River Thames to the former abbey beyond.

West Wycombe Park and Caves (p. 179), Buckinghamshire
SU 830 948, Landranger Sheet 175
The house and grounds are in the care of the National Trust but the nearby caves are still run as an attraction by the Dashwood family.

Whittlesford Church (p. 150), Cambs
TL 473 485, Landranger Sheet 154
The carving is located above the main entrance to Whittlesford Church 7 miles south of Cambridge.

SOUTH-WEST

Avebury Stone Circle (p. 40), Wiltshire
SU 103 700, Landranger Sheet 173
The circle encloses the entire village of Avebury. Visitor parking is well signposted and within walking distance of the stones.

Barbara Hepworth Gallery (p. 225), Cornwall
SW 517 407, Landranger Sheet 203
Trewyn Studio, St Ives is open to the public.

Avebury henge circle.

Bath Roman Baths (p. 116), Somerset
ST 761 634, Landranger Sheet 172
Within Bath city centre the site is well signposted.

Bennett's Cross (p. 139), Devon
SX 679 816, Landranger Sheet 191
A short walk from the road across Dartmoor. An Ordnance
Survey map may be required to find this site.

Boleigh Fogou (p. 79), Cornwall
SW 438 252, Landranger Sheet 203
The fogou lies in the grounds of a private house and is only
accessible by arrangement.

Carn Euny Fogou (p. 79), Cornwall
SW 403 288, Landranger Sheet 203
Two miles south-west of the village of Sancreed the road peters
out and Carn Euny is signposted from here.

Cerne Abbas Giant (p. 2), chalk figure, Dorset
ST 666 017, Landranger Sheet 194
The figure lies to the north of the village of Cerne Abbas on
Giant Hill. The former gardens of Lord Holles lie in pasture at
the foot of the hill and there is a public right of way through this
field.

Eden Project (p. 223), sculptures, Cornwall
SX 050 550, Landranger Sheet 200
Near St Austell and well signposted.

Glastonbury Tor (p. 89), sacred hill, Somerset
ST 512 386, Landranger Sheet 183
Finding the Tor is not difficult as it is visible from miles around.

Glendurgan Gardens (p. 208), Cornwall
SW 773 274, Landranger Sheet 204
On the coast 3 miles south-west of Falmouth.

Halliggye Fogou (p. 79), Cornwall
SW 713 239, Landranger Sheet 203

The Hurlers (p. 33), stone circle complex, Cornwall
Centred SX 258 714, Landranger Sheet 201
Just north of Minions village is a tall structure
– formerly a tin mine and now a museum. Keeping the
museum on your right, walk 500 metres onto the moor
to find the stone circles.

Lansdown Tower (p. 205), Somerset
ST 736 676, Landranger Sheet 172
Also known as Beckford's Tower, this lies to the north of the city
of Bath and is open to the public. Beckford's former residence,
Fonthill Abbey, is in private ownership and not open to the
public.

Long Tom (p. 140), standing stone, Cornwall
SX 255 706, Landranger Sheet 201
On a minor road to the south-west of Minions village.

Lost Gardens of Heligan (p. 229), sculpture, Cornwall
SW 997 465, Landranger Sheet 204
Three miles south of St Austell.

Marlborough Mound (p. 92), Wiltshire
SU 184 686, Landranger Sheet 173
The Mound now lies in the grounds of Marlborough College but
access is negotiable.

Men-an-Tol (p. 46), standing stones, Cornwall
SW 426 349, Landranger Sheet 203
Remains of wider stone setting, two upright pillars and a holed
stone. A rough track leads from the main road onto open
moorland. The stones are just over half a mile's walk from the
road on the right hand side, sometimes hidden from view by
vegetation.

Glastonbury Tor.

241

Rocky Valley (p. 89), carved cliff, Cornwall
SX 073 893, Landranger Sheet 200
A footpath leads down Rocky Valley from the road to the coast. The carvings are clearly indicated on the right.

St Augustine's Well (p. 141), natural water source and votive pool, Dorset
ST 665 013, Landranger Sheet 194
The well is concealed within trees behind the village church.

Saint Piran's Cross (p. 139), Cornwall
SW 773 564, Landranger Sheet 200
Situated on Penhale Sands near Perranporth.

The Sanctuary (p. 39), ritual site, Wiltshire
SU 119 680, Landranger Sheet 173
The site lies adjacent to the main road between Marlborough and Beckhampton on the route of the ancient Ridgeway. Although no stones or wooden posts survive, their former positions are marked in concentric rings and the view west to Silbury Hill and the West Kennet burial mound is worth the visit alone.

Silbury Hill (p. 94), artificial mound, Wiltshire
SU 100 685, Landranger Sheet 173
There is no direct access to Silbury Hill itself but the mound can be seen from roadside viewing areas and a footpath circumnavigates the monument at a distance.

Stonehenge (p. 35), earthwork henge and stone circle, Wiltshire
SU 122 422, Landranger Sheet 184
Stonehenge is in the care of English Heritage.

Stourhead (p. 191), landscape gardens, Wiltshire
ST 780 344, Landranger Sheet 183
In the ownership of the National Trust.

Tintagel Castle and Monastery (p. 159), Cornwall
SX 049 892, Landranger Sheet 200
In the care of English Heritage.

West Kennet (p. 49), chambered long barrow, Wiltshire
SU 105 677, Landranger Sheet 173
Access is by means of a footpath from the north. It is possible to enter the barrow interior.

West Kennet Avenue (p. 40), stone avenue, Wiltshire
From SU 119 680 to SU 103 700, Landranger Sheet 173
Runs between Overton Hill and Avebury Stone Circle. Not all of the stones survive in place but it is possible to walk much of the length of the avenue.

Wimble Toot, barrow, Somerset
ST 561 280, Landranger Sheet 183
In farmland near Babcary.

Zennor Church (p. 152), carvings, Cornwall
SW 455 385 Landranger Sheet 203

SCOTLAND

MAINLAND
Aikey Brae (p. 15), recumbent stone circle, Aberdeenshire
NJ 958 471, Landranger Sheet 30
Leave the road on a tight bend where a grassed-over track heads up hill. A pathway has now been made through the field to a plantation. Aikey Brae lies on the other side of the trees.

Anstruther Beach (p. 194), Fife
NO 565 030, Landranger Sheet 59
This is a public beach with unrestricted access.

Tintagel Castle.

Ballochmyle Wall (p. 107), prehistoric rock art site, Ayrshire
NS 511 255, Landranger Sheet 70
Rock art wall near the village of Mauchline between Kingencleugh Castle and Ballochmyle golf club. The wall lies off the main pathway just a short walk from the nearby viaduct.

Balnuaran (p. 70), cairns, Highland
NH 757 444, Landranger Sheet 27
The burial complex of Balnuaran lies on the flood plain of the River Nairn 4 miles due east of Inverness and is well sign posted.

Cairnbaan (p. 104), prehistoric rock art site, Argyll and Bute
NR 839 911, Landranger Sheet 55
Cup-and ring marked stones signposted from the main road and a short, steep walk uphill. The extensive rock art site of Achnabreck also lies nearby on the other side of the valley, centred at NR 858 905.

A Chioch (p. 86), the Breast, natural hill, Highland
NO 093 987, Landranger Sheet 43
In the Cairngorm Mountains.

Chioch Mor, the Big Breast, **Chioch Bheag**, the Little Breast, **Beinn Cichean** (p. 85) – peaks on Lochnagar, the Mountain of Teats
NO 260 861 and NO 265 844, Aberdeenshire Landranger Sheet 44

Cothiemuir Wood (p. 20), recumbent stone circle, Aberdeenshire
NJ 617 198, Landranger Sheet 37
Finding Cothiemuir Wood requires a little navigating. At a tight dogleg bend in the road, strike off due west for a couple of hundred metres. The stones can be seen in a clearing in the trees.

Culsh (p. 78), souterrain, Aberdeenshire
NJ 505 055, Landranger Sheet 37
Dug into a grassy slope right by the road just east of Tarland. There is free access to explore this underground tunnel.

Dunchraigaig (p. 57), cairn, Argyll and Bute
NR 833 968, Landranger Sheet 55
The cairn lies just to the west of the main road a little over 1 mile south of Kilmartin village.

Earlshall Gardens (p. 218), Fife
NO 464 210, Landranger Sheet 59
Earlshall house and gardens, behind RAF Leuchars, are in private ownership but the grounds are accessible to the public on occasional open days.

Garbh Chioch Bheag, the Small, Rough Breast, and **Garbh Chioch Mhor**, the Big, Rough Breast (p. 85), natural hills between Loch Nevis and Loch Quoich in the Highland region
NM 925 956 and NM 909 962, Landranger Sheet 40

Glenquickan (p. 24), stone circle, Dumfries and Galloway
NX 509 582, Landranger 83
Leaving the single-track road near a stream, the stone circle lies one field due south of the road.

Grey Cairns of Camster (p. 67), horned cairn, Highland
ND 260 442, Landranger Sheet 11 or 12
A single-track road runs straight between the settlements of Watten (10 miles west of Wick) and Lybster on the coast. The Camster Cairns are visible roughly half way along this road, to the west.

Kellie Castle (p. 217), Fife
NO 520 052, Landranger Sheet 59
The castle and gardens at Kellie are open to the public and cared for by Historic Scotland.

Balnuaran cup marks.

Kintraw cairn and standing stone.

Kintraw (p. 58), cairn and standing stone, Argyll and Bute
NM 830 050, Landranger Sheet 55
Standing stone and cairn five miles north of Kilmartin. The stone is visible on the inland side of the road on a tight bend above Loch Craignish.

Loanhead of Daviot (p. 17), recumbent stone circle, Aberdeenshire
NJ 747 288, Landranger Sheet 38
The village of Daviot lies 4 miles north west of Inverurie. The stone circle is located on raised ground at the north of the village, not far from the cemetery.

Maiden Paps (p. 85), natural hillocks, Borders
NT 500 024, Landranger Sheet 79
Approximately 10 miles south of Hawick.

Maiden Paps (p. 85), natural glacial mounds, Dumbarton
Centred NS 501 756, Landranger Sheet 64
These mounds can be found on the south side of Loch Cochno to the north of Bearsden, a western district of Glasgow.

Mither Tap (p. 86), natural hill, Aberdeenshire
NJ 682 224, Landranger Sheet 38
Pyramid-shaped hill dominating the horizon at the east end of the Bennachie range of hills.

Sgorr Na Ciche or the Pap of Glencoe (p. 85), Highland
NN 125 595, Landranger Sheet 41
This peak rises at the entrance to Glencoe.

Tap o'Noth (p. 86), natural hill, Aberdeenshire
NJ 484 294, Landranger Sheet 37

Tom Na Grugaich, the Maidens' Hillock (p. 85), natural hill, Highland

NG 859 602, Landranger Sheet 24
On the stunning mountain of Ben Alligin in Torridon.

Whitehill (p. 17), recumbent stone circle, Aberdeenshire
NJ 643 135, Landranger Sheet 37
Take the forestry track uphill to the east of Tillyfourie. The circle is signposted.

ORKNEY
Cuween (p. 54), chambered tomb, Orkney
HY 365 128, Landranger Sheet 6
Less than 1 mile south of Finstown and an opposite extreme to the commercially run tomb of Maes Howe. A rough track leads up to the grassy mound but the last section is a steep walk uphill so it is free from the tourist groups that make a bee-line for Maes Howe. A torch is recommended for exploring the tomb.

Maes Howe (p. 59), chambered tomb, Orkney
HY 318 128, Landranger Sheet 6
Entry to Maes Howe is by guided tour from Tormiston Mill, which contains an interesting museum and visitor centre.

Mine Howe (p. 77), underground chamber, Orkney
HY 515 061, Landranger Sheet 6
Less than 2 miles south-east of Kirkwall Airport. There is a small visitor centre with a fascinating display charting the re-discovery of the chamber.

Ring of Brodgar (p. 31), stone circle, Orkney
HY 294 133, Landranger Sheet 6
Signposted from the main Stromness to Kirkwall road on the Ness of Brodgar.

Skara Brae (p. 31), prehistoric village, Orkney
HY 229 188, Landranger Sheet 6
One of the most exciting prehistoric sites in Britain situated on the west coast by the Bay of Skaill.

Stones of Stenness (p. 46), stone circle, Orkney
HY 306 125, Landranger Sheet 6
Less than 1 mile south-east of the Ring of Brodgar, the stones are visible on the east side of the road.

WESTERN ISLES
Callanish Tursachan (p. 29), monolith, stone circle and avenues, Isle of Lewis
NB 213 330, Landranger Sheet 13
The stones lie between the shore and the main west coast road, locally signed Calanais.

Cnoc Fillibhear Bheag (p. 28), stone circle, Isle of Lewis
NB 225 326, Landranger Sheet 13
This site (pronounced 'Craw Fillyver Vegg') stands on a plateau of high ground within sight of Callanish Tursachan. The path to the stones can be very boggy even in summer.

Loch Conailbhe (p. 99), sacred Loch of the Goddess, Islay
NR 215 600, Landranger Sheet 60
A small expanse of water just half a mile east of Kilchiaran on the west coast of the island.

Machrie Moor (p. 21), stone circle complex, Arran
NR 910 324, Landranger Sheet 69
From a gateway less than half a mile north of Tormore on the west coast of Arran, a rough track leads inland and uphill from the main road for about 1 mile onto open moorland with unrestricted access.

Mullach Dubh (p. 83), standing stone, Islay
NR 404 642, Landranger Sheet 60
The stone stands within open farmed pasture just over 1 mile south of the village of Ballygrant. A very rough track leads to within sight of the stone.

Ritual Cave site (p. 75), Isle of Eigg
NM 492 898, Landranger Sheet 39

Sgurr Nan Gilean (p. 85), Peak of the Young Men, Cuillins, Isle of Skye
NG 472 253, Landranger Sheet 32

WALES

Bryn-Celli-Ddu (p. 57), chambered burial mound, Anglesey, Gwynedd
SH 507 702 Landranger Sheet 115
Prehistoric tomb near the village of Llanddaniel Fab, 2 miles south-west of the Britannia Bridge on the island's main coastal route.

Harold's Stones (p. 14), triple standing stones, Gwent
SO 499 052, Landranger Sheet 162
Passing through the village of Trellech, five miles south of Monmouth, the stones are clearly visible.

St Illtud's Priory Church (p. 140), Pembrokeshire
SS 141 963, Landranger Sheet 158
Caldey Island in Carmarthen Bay is a short ferry ride from Tenby on the mainland. St Illtud's Church can be found near the modern monastery there.

Samson's Jack (p. 13), standing stone, West Glamorgan
SS 476 923, Landranger Sheet 159
The pillar stands in a hedgerow near Windmill Farm on the Gower Peninsula. It lies within private farmland so permission is required from the farm before visiting.

JERSEY

Le Pinacle (p. 101), natural rock formation, Jersey
Le Pinacle rises from the rocky shore in the north-west of the

Cnoc Fillibhear Bheag.

245

The Paps of Anu.

island, just south of a structure known as the German Tower between Grosnez Point and Grande Etacquerel.

IRELAND

Kilsarken (p. 148, exhibitionist carving, County Kerry
R 027 018, Sheet 72
The ruins of Kilsarken church can be found to the east of Farranfore on north-facing slopes overlooking the valley of the Brown Flesk River. When visiting, please be mindful that this is still a functioning cemetery for the local area.

Knowth (p. 65), passage tomb, Bru na Boine, County Meath
N 996 734 Sheet 43
Access to Knowth is via a well signposted Visitor Centre on the minor road that follows the south side of the River Boyne between Slane and Drogheda.

Loughcrew (p. 61), passage tomb, County Meath
N 586 776, Sheet 42
Cairn T lies on the hill of Slieve na Calliagh 7 miles south of Oldcastle.

Lough Nageeha (p. 100), sacred lake, County Kerry
W 126 862, Sheet 79
Descending northwards a short distance down the 'cleavage' between the Paps of Anu, Lough Nageeha can be seen below. Care should be taken as the gully quickly becomes too steep to continue and the ground here is unstable underfoot.

Mount Mapas (p. 201), monument, Dublin
O 261 255, Discovery Series Sheet 50
On the summit of Killiney Hill 8 miles south-east of Dublin city centre. There are paths leading up to the monument with stunning views along the coast.

Newgrange (p. 64), passage tomb, Bru na Boine, County Meath
O 007 727 Sheet 43
Access to Newgrange is via the Visitor Centre on a minor road that follows the south side of the River Boyne between Slane and Drogheda.

The Paps of Anu (p. 89), paired hills, County Kerry
W 125 855 and W 134 855, Sheet 79
The best views of the Paps are from the north-west. There are no formal footpaths onto the hills and the climb up is a steep one.

Rath Riogh (p. 136), enclosure, and **Lia Fail**, standing stone, County Meath
N 920 597, Sheet 42
On the Hill of Tara, 20 miles north-west of Dublin.

Turoe Stone (p. 134), decorated pillar, Galway
M 626 225 Sheet 46
Located at Turoe Farm 3.5 miles north of Loughrea. Visitors are welcome and facilities are provided.